100 … DAM

100% AMSTERDAM

"Valiant, steadfast, compassionate" is the official motto of the city of Amsterdam. Nowadays, you could make that friendly, surprising and multicultural. In 'Mokum', as the locals call their city, there really is never a dull moment. So where to start? Shopping, a dip into the city's culture or a nice meal? Amsterdam has everything: unique shops in the Negen Straatjes (9 Little Streets), modern architecture on de eilanden (the islands), Holland's best travel book shop in chic Oud-Zuid (Old South) and the best ice cream in town in De Pijp district. And everywhere you'll come across trendy restaurants, happening clubs and the typically Amsterdam cosy 'brown cafés'. In no time, this guide will bring you to the places you'll want to see. Sightseeing, shopping, a culinary or cultural experience, or an adventure: wherever you want to be, our clear maps show you the way.

100% AMSTERDAM, DISCOVER THE CITY IN NO-TIME!

Table of content

100% Transparent

To make this guide easy to read, we've divided Amsterdam into 6 interesting areas. For each area we provide a detailed map. The general map on the first page gives an overview showing where the 6 areas are located. The letters (A) t/m (W) mark places of interest, hotels and restaurants described in the guide that fall outside the 6 areas.

The 6 area chapters give detailed descriptions of what each area has to offer, its main sights, good places for a drink, a meal, shopping or simply relaxing. Each address is tagged with a number (1) that you'll find on the map at the end of the chapter. The colour code tells you where to find the description and what type of attraction it is:

● places of interest	● shopping
● food & drinks	● fun things to do

6 WALKS

Each chapter also contains a walk of about three hours marked on the map. The walk is described on the page next to the map, and takes in some of the most interesting and attractive places in the city, including some less well-known. So you miss out on nothing: wonderful sights, museums, parks and shops, and great eateries ranging from informal cafés to smart restaurants. Of course, if you don't feel like walking the route, you can still use the descriptions and maps to explore the city or simply to check up on places where you just happen to find yourself.

NATIONAL HOLIDAYS

As well as movable feast days such as Easter, Ascension Day and Pentecost, the Dutch have the following additional public holidays:

1st January	- New Year's Day
30th April	- Queen's Day
25th & 26th December	- Christmas

FESTIVALS

All over Amsterdam there are annual festivals, mainly in the summer. Listed below is a selection of some of the bigger events:

Amsterdam Roots: world music festival. June. Oosterpark & other locations. *www.amsterdamroots.nl*

Over het IJ Festival: theatre in Amsterdam-Noord. July. NDSM-werf. *www.overhetij.nl*

Holland Festival: experimental music, opera, theatre and dance. May & June. Stadsschouwburg and other locations. *www.hollandfestival.nl*

Theater Amsterdamse Bos: open air theatre. July & August. Amsterdamse Bos. *www.bostheater.nl*

Kwakoe Festival: multicultural festival. 6 weekends in July & August. Bijlmerpark. *www.kwakoe.nl*

Gay Pride Parade: canal parade with extravagant costumes. Early August. Prinsengracht & other locations. *www.amsterdampride.nl*

De Parade: travelling theatre festival. First half August. Martin Luther King Park. *www.deparade.nl*

Grachtenfestival: classical music. August. Various locations, including on canal pontoons. *www.grachtenfestival.nl*

Uitmarkt: launch of the cultural season. Last weekend in August. Leidseplein, Museumplein & other locations. *www.uitmarkt.nl*

IDFA: international documentary festival. November. De Balie & other locations. *www.idfa.nl*

Hartjesdagen: small festival with folk music, street performances, operetta and ending with the drag costume 'hearts parade' on and around the Zeedijk. August. *www.hartjesdagen.nl*

INDICATION OF PRICES FOR HOTELS AND RESTAURANTS

With hotel and restaurant contact details of, we provide a price indication. Unless otherwise stated, rates per hotel are based on a double room per night and rates for restaurants on the average price for a main course.

DO YOU HAVE TIPS?

Our research is thorough and our local know-how extensive. We also try to be as accurate as possible when putting this guide together. But shops and restaurants in particular change frequently in Amsterdam (that's part of what makes it so dynamic!). So if you can't find one a listed address or have comments or tips for us, please let us know at *www.100procentamsterdam.nl.* On this Dutch website, we also give updates and additions to the guide and for events organised in the city.

Please note that none of the selected addresses have paid for texts or pictures to be in this guide, which has been written by a staff of independent authors and editors.

VONDELKERK

Hotels

Amsterdam is a city that has something for everyone and that equally true of its hotels. With a few hundred addresses to choose from, the selection is generous. Looking for something modern or prefer the nostalgic? Big or small? It's all to be found in Amsterdam. The rates vary from € 23.50 for a bed in a youth hostel to sky-high rates for a night in a five star hotel. For a room in a three-star hotel you'll typically pay around € 120. Alongside the well-known chains and mid-range hotels, Amsterdam also offers some very special accommodation. More information can of course be found on the internet and looking out for attractive offers is definitely worth your while.

Some websites:
www.expedia.nl and *www.booking.com* are two websites where you can find hotels in various price ranges. *www.sfeerhotels.nl* has an overview of special hotels in, amongst other places, Amsterdam.
www.amsterdam-accommodation.nl is good if you're looking for apartments or Bed & Breakfasts. *www.amsterdamtourist.nl* is the official site of the Amsterdam Tourism and Convention Board and provides information about the city, including hotels and other accommodation.

Listed below we describe a few of the more special hotels in different price ranges. The letters correspond to the map in the front of the guide. Unless otherwise specified, rates are for a double room for one night excluding breakfast.

BUDGET

(A) Amongst all the dingy hotels on warmoesstraat, Hotel **Winston** comes as a pleasant surprise. This artistic hotel, now also known as a 'St. Christopher's Inn', is dedicated to art. Eight of the 67 rooms have been designed by artists. The Heineken room has become the hotel's most popular. The built-in night-club Winston Kingdom with its live music is also something of a hotspot.
warmoesstraat 129, phone 020 623 13 80, www.winston.nl, rates from € 75, tram 4, 9, 16, 24, 25 dam square

LLOYD HOTEL (F)

(B) Nowhere will you make international friends more easily than in the **Stayokay Vondelpark**. This excellent youth hostel is located on the edge of Vondelpark and offers rooms for every budget: cheap dormitories through to more expensive rooms. Perfectly situated close to Leidseplein and only a short walk from the Rijksmuseum.
zandpad 5, phone 020 589 89 96, www.stayokay.nl, rates from € 23.50 p.p./p.n. (dorms), tram 1, 2, 5 leidseplein

(C) Those looking for something different can do worse than overnight on a boat on the river Amstel. The **Amstel Botel** offers 175 comfortable single, double and triple rooms, each with private bathroom. If you've stayed here before, take note: the Botel has recently moved to the NDSM-pier, but remains within easy walking distance of Central Station.
NDSM-pier 3, phone 020 521 03 50, www.amstelbotel.nl, rates from € 78, tram 1, 2, 4, 5, 9, 13, 16, 24, 25 central station

(D) **Bicycle Hotel Van Ostade**, as the name suggests, is a bicycle hotel where you can stay the night and store or rent a bike. The friendly owners of this simple but clean hotel are only to glad to help you explore the city. The hotel has sixteen standard rooms, a breakfast room next to a small garden and is located in the trendy Pijp district.
van ostadestraat 123, phone 020 679 34 52, www.bicyclehotel.com, rates from € 50, tram 24, 25 ceintuurbaan

MID-RANGE

(E) Hotel **De Filosoof** is situated in a quiet area close to Vondelpark, with a spacious garden, bar and 38 special rooms. Each room is decorated according to a different philosophical theme! The Confucius room, for example, with its deep purple colours and light furniture, is dedicated to Confucius' Chinese philosophy and Taoism. Other rooms are dedicated to greats such as Spinoza, Nietzsche and Wittgenstein or have themes such as passion, clouds and water.
anna van den vondelstraat 6, phone 020 683 30 13, www.hoteldefilosoof.nl, rates from € 95, tram 1 jan pieter heijestraat

(F) The **Lloyd Hotel** on Oostelijke Handelskade is a beautifully renovated listed building. This remarkable hotel has 120 innovatively designed rooms, varying in luxury from one to five stars. No two rooms are the same. There's a pleasant lobby restaurant, where they offer both simple and more extensive menus. You'll also find a cultural embassy and a library here.
oostelijke handelskade 34, phone 020 561 36 36, www.lloydhotel.com, rates from € 110, bus 43 lloydplein, tram 10 azartplein

(G) **Hotel Arena** will always be one of the most remarkable hotels in town. This listed building not only houses a trendy accommodation for travellers, but also houses a popular nightclub. On Friday and Saturday nights especially, they're going wild in the former chapel that is now Club Tonight. The 121 hotel rooms are decorated in a minimalist style with design classics. Private parking facilities are available (€25 per 24 hours). The hotel is due to become somewhat more luxurious and expensive.
's-gravesandestraat, phone 020 850 24 20, www.hotelarena.nl, rates from € 100, tram 9, 14 sarphatistraat/tropenmuseum

(H) **Hotel V** has recently opened at a second location. Both are excellent and affordable boutique hotels offering free wifi, cow hide furniture, a modern interior, fun surprises dotted about and even Apple computers in the lounge. The one hotel is located on Victorieplein at the southern edge of the Pijp area, the other, newer hotel is even closer to the city centre at Frederiksplein. Hip and fun!
victorieplein 42 and weteringschans 136, phone 020 662 32 33, www.hotelv.nl, rates from € 99, tram 4, 12, 25 victorieplein and tram 4, 7, 10 weteringschans

(I) **The College Hotel** is the place to be for Amsterdam's more stylish visitor. Located in a 19th century school building in Oud Zuid (Old South) area, the hotel has very modern and comfortable rooms, excellent service, and a pleasant terrace. In the very popular hotel bar guests rub shoulders with the local yuppie clientele. The College Restaurant, with its classic Dutch cuisine, is very good.
roelof hartstraat 1, phone 020 571 15 11, www.collegehotelamsterdam.com, rates from € 175, tram 2, 3, 12 roelof hartplein

Ⓖ **HOTEL ARENA**

TOP END

(J) The **Grand Hotel Amrâth** is the newest five star hotel in town. Situated in the impressive, old Scheepvaarthuis (Shipping House), this beautiful hotel is an oasis of tranquillity and, above all, luxury. Discover the numerous exquisite architectural details or enjoy free drinks from the mini-bar and Nespresso machines (both are included in the room rate). The Wellness Centre, the top restaurant Seven Seas and the beautiful bar are the complement to a luxurious weekend in Amsterdam.
prins hendrikkade 108, phone 020 552 00 00, www.amrathamsterdam.com, rates from € 475 (check special offers), tram 1, 2, 4, 5, 9, 13, 16, 24, 25 central station

(K) **Hotel 717** is located in a beautiful, green-shuttered canal house. An oak staircase leads up from the marble hall to the eight luxurious suites, two of which overlook the canal with six looking out over the small garden.
prinsengracht 717, phone 020 427 07 17, www.717hotel.nl, rates from € 375, tram 10, 17 elandsgracht

(L) A true Amsterdam classic, the **American Hotel** (pronounced 'Americain') was built in 1902 and is renowned for its great service and beautiful rooms overlooking Leidseplein. The hotel has recently been refurbished and has a wonderful terrace. The charming art deco-style Café American remains for Amsterdammers, too, a treasured spot for a read, to catch a bite or to enjoy the Sunday brunch. The hotel is also popular with rock stars performing at the nearby Paradiso or Melkweg music venues.
leidsekade 97, phone 020 556 30 00, www.amsterdamamerican.nl, rates from € 200, tram 1, 2, 5 leidseplein

Transport

The easiest way to reach Amsterdam is by **train**. From Central Station, where work is in progress on a new metro line due to open in 2012, it's a simple stroll straight into town.

If you're arriving by **car**, it's best to park at a so-called **P+R** (Park + Ride). This means leaving your car at the Amsterdam ArenA stadium, Sloterdijk railway station, Zeeburger Island or old Olympic stadium on the four edges of town and then transferring to public transport. It costs € 6 per 24 hours (maximum 96 hour stay), including two return tickets for public transport. In the city centre you pay up to € 4 per hour between 9.00 am and midnight. The exact charges can be found at *www.parkerenamsterdam.nl* (Dutch only).

In the city centre, it's safest to park in one of the official **car parks**, where prices vary up to € 4 per hour. **On-street parking** charges differ by area from € 1.30 to € 4 per hour, with costs generally higher the closer to the centre you park. **Daily and weekly parking passes** valid throughout the city are available at the various 'Stadstoezicht' service points.

The best way to get around within the city is by **tram**. Amsterdam has sixteen tram lines, most leaving Central Station for the East, South or West of the city. Tram 26 runs on a solitary route from Central Station out to the recently redeveloped former docklands Oostelijke Eilanden (Eastern Islands) and IJburg districts. Other tram lines cover the older city areas and neighbourhoods.

The bus is a convenient way to get from Central Station to more outlaying parts of the city, such as Amsterdam Noord (North). After midnight, there are **night buses** operating via or from Central Station.

Trains on Amsterdam's **metro** service run less frequently than metro systems in many major cities (up to 8 times an hour in rush hour, less frequently outside peak times). Lines 53 and 54 connect Central Station with the Zuidoost (South-East) business district. Line 51 runs from Central Station via Buitenveldert to the adjacent town of Amstelveen, while line 50 runs from Amsterdam Sloterdijk train station to Gein via Zuid (South) train station.

Important: For buses, trams and the metro you need a '**strippenkaart**' (strip card). The number of strips you need for each journey = the number of zones you're traveling through + one. You can check the number of zones you're travelling using the table on the route network map posted at every stop. If you don't have a strip card, you can buy a (much more expensive) ticket from the tram or bus driver or conductor. For the metro you'll need to buy your ticket from the machines in the hall of the metro station. Amsterdam intends to introduce the 'OV-chipkaart' in 2009. This is a chip-based travel card that comes in three forms: personal, anonymous and disposable, and is valid in the tram, metro and bus.

You can hail any **taxi** on the street and there are several taxi stands around town. The phone number of the best-known taxi company, TCA, is 020 677 77 77. The maximum taxi fare for up to four passengers is a flat rate € 7.50, which includes the first two kilometres, plus a maximum € 2.20 per kilometre thereafter. Ask the driver beforehand what the total fare will be and to switch on his meter.

One of the most pleasant ways to get round the city centre is the hop-on, hop-off **Canal Bus**. This regular service runs along three routes through Amsterdam's canals with fourteen stops all close to the important museums, shopping areas and other places of interest. With a day ticket (€ 20, valid until 12.00 noon the next day), you can simply hop on and off any Canal Bus all day long. There's also on-board commentary on passing sites. More information can be found at *www.canal.nl*.

You can also tour the canals in one of the many **canal boats** for hire at Rokin (a street name) or discover Amsterdam the Dutch way: by **bike**! There are several bike rental shops dotted across town. See *www.rent-a-bike.nl*, *www.macbike.nl* or *www.bikecity.nl* for more information.

Relatively new is the **bike taxi**. Mainly found in the city centre, it can offer a romantic or convenient option for short distances. You're charged € 1 per person per three minutes. And you may even come across one of the genuine Thai **Tuk Tuk** mini-taxis now entering the Dutch urban landscape. Great fun! To book a Tuk Tuk call 0900 993 33 99.

City centre

This is Amsterdam as the world knows it. In the old city centre you get a real sense of the historic heart and soul of this beautiful city: its early origins, its changes, its later wealth. Amsterdam has some of the oldest canals and churches that attract tourists from all over the world. Grand canal houses mix it with the world-famous of the red light district, though the city council would now like to see somewhat less of the latter and is working hard to make this area, arguably the most beautiful part of Amsterdam, more appealing.

The streets around the Oude Kerk (Old Church) are the oldest part of the city centre, dating back to the Middle Ages when the city thrived on its herring and beer trade.

1

All that changed during the Golden Age when along the canals, majestic buildings rose up with large courtyards and the Kalverstraat was transformed from a dusty cattle market into a chic shopping street.

The most dynamic areas of the old city centre are Chinatown and Nieuwmarkt (New Market). The Zeedijk, in particular, has several Asian shops and eateries appealing to people of all cultures and tastes. So don't let the drunken British tourists scare you off. There's more than enough to explore here. And don't forget the canal boat tours, the theatres on the narrow street, Nes, as well as the countless shops.

6x what not to miss!

Royal Palace

Visit the Royal Palace on Dam Square.

Puccini

Buy pepper chocolates at Puccini.

Oudemanhuispoort

Stroll through the Oudemanhuispoort.

Café Bern

Have a cheese fondue at Café Bern.

Red-light district

Wander through the red-light district at night.

Comedy Theatre

Enjoy a night out at the Comedy Theatre on Nes.

- **Places of interest**
- **Shopping**
- **Food & drinks**
- **Fun things to do**

Places of interest

(3) The **National Monument on Dam Square** was built in 1956 in remembrance of the Dutchmen who died in World War II. The semi-circular remembrance wall behind the pillar displays a text by Dutch poet A. Roland Holst.
dam, tram 4, 9, 16, 24, 25 dam

(4) Though the **Royal Palace** on Dam Square is still in use for official functions, it normally has (limited) opening hours for the public, though at the time of writing, renovations were in progress with it due to reopen in 2009. The building is simple and sombre from the outside, but inside it's quite spectacular. Free guided tours are available on Wednesday and Sunday afternoon at 2pm.
dam 1, phone 020 620 40 60, www.kon-paleisamsterdam.nl, opening hours vary, admission adults € 4.50, children age 6-16 € 3.60, tram 4, 9, 16, 24, 25 dam

(5) The **Nieuwe Kerk** (New Church) was built at the beginning of the 15th century as a second church after the Oude Kerk (Old Church). Nowadays major art and photo exhibitions are regularly held here. It is also the church where current Crown Prince Willem-Alexander and Princess Máxima got married on 2nd February 2002.
gravenstraat 17, phone 020 638 69 09, www.nieuwekerk.nl, opening hours vary (only during exhibitions), admission varies, tram 4, 9, 16, 24, 25 dam

(9) The **Oudemanhuispoort** is a roof-covered passage joining Oudezijds Achterburgwal to Kloveniersburgwal. The gate used to lead to the Oudemannen- en Vrouwengasthuis (old men and women's hospital), but now leads to the main building of the University of Amsterdam. You'll find plenty of students here, drawn by the stalls selling second-hand books and magazines.
oudemanhuispoort, open mon-sat 12.00-18.00, tram 4, 9, 16, 24, 25 muntplein

(15) A visit to the **Rembrandthuis** (Rembrandt's house) gives a good impression of the place where this great painter lived and worked between 1639 and 1658. In one of the wings of the museum some of his paintings, etchings and drawings are on display.
jodenbreestraat 4, phone 020 520 04 00, www.rembrandthuis.nl, open mon-sat 10.00-17.00, admission adults € 8, children age 6-15 € 1.50, tram 9, 14 waterlooplein

(26) The **Fo Guang Shan He Hua Temple** is the largest Chinese Buddhist temple in Europe. It is used for Buddhist ceremonies and you can attend courses in Chinese and Buddhism. Guided tours are available daily except Sundays (reservations required).
zeedijk 106-118, phone 020 420 23 57, www.ibps.nl, open tue-sat 12.00-17.00, sun 10.00-17.00, free, tram 1, 2, 4, 5, 9, 13, 16, 17, 24, 25 central station

(32) Hidden away in the attic of this canal house, is a tiny church **Ons' Lieve Heer op Solder** (Our Lord in the Attic), built in the 17th century because official churches were Protestant and Catholics were only allowed to hold services in places not formally recognised as churches.
oudezijdse voorburgwal 40, phone 020 624 66 04, www.museumamstelkring.nl, open mon-sat 10.00-17.00, sun and public holidays 13.00-17.00, admission adults € 7, children age 5-18 € 1, children age 0-4 free, tram 1, 2, 4, 5, 9, 13, 16, 17, 24, 25 central station

(33) The **Oude Kerk** (Old Church) is Amsterdam's oldest monument and has since been named a European Monument. Exhibitions and concerts are regularly held here.
oudekerksplein 23, phone 020 625 82 84, www.oudekerk.nl, open mon-sat 11.00-17.00, sun 13.00-17.00, admission € 5, tram 1, 2, 4, 5, 9, 13, 16, 17, 24, 25 central station

NATIONAAL MONUMENT OP DE DAM 3

10

2

8

Places to eat & drink

(2) At the **Bakkerswinkel** (Baker's shop) you can get a healthy breakfast or lunch of delicious made-to-order sandwiches, or enjoy sweet and savoury pies, cakes and scones. The trendy yet snug interior has been partly designed by furniture designer Piet Hein Eek.
warmoesstraat 69, phone 020 489 80 00, www.bakkerswinkel.nl, open tue-fri 08.00-18.00, sat 08.00-17.00, sun 10.00-17.00, price € 12, tram 1, 2, 4, 5, 9, 13, 16, 17, 24, 25 central station

(8) Tucked away in the alley Gebed zonder End (Endless Prayer) is bar-restaurant **Kapitein Zeppos** where you enjoy a drink, lunch or dinner in a friendly atmosphere. This is a great, hidden-away location that occasionally hosts good live performances.
gebed zonder end 5, phone 020 624 20 57, open mon-thu 11.00-01.00, fri 11.00-15.00, sat 11.00-01.00, sun 12.00-01.00, price € 26, tram 4, 9, 16, 24, 25 rokin

(10) The superb terrace overlooking the river Amstel has been one reason for the enduring popularity of grand café **De Jaren**. In the summer, you should count yourself lucky if you find an empty seat on the terrace. Inside, the large, open plan and minimalist interior also offers a very pleasant spot for a drink or meal.
nieuwe doelenstraat 20/22, phone 020 625 57 71, open mon-thu, sun 10.00-01.00, fri-sat 10.00-02.00, price € 24, tram 4, 9, 16, 24, 25 muntplein

(11) The five stars of **Hotel de l'Europe** scares many people off, but if you have the nerve, do go in, if only to visit Freddy's Bar. According to Dutch newspaper Het Parool, this is the best hotel bar in Amsterdam and named after the legendary brewer, Freddy Heineken, who even had his own telephone there (it's still there).
nieuwe doelenstraat 2-8, phone 020 531 17 77, www.leurope.nl, open daily 11.00-01.00, tram 4,9, 16, 24, 25 muntplein

(20) **Café Bern** on Nieuwmarkt (New Market) is synonymous with the tastiest cheese fondue in Amsterdam. But the entrecote, which you cook yourself at the table, definitely holds its own. Ideally, you should order both; and that's what most of the regulars do.
nieuwmarkt 9, phone 020 622 00 34, open daily 18.00-00.00, price € 15, tram 1, 2, 4, 5, 9, 13, 16, 17, 24, 25 central station

(21) A little piece of Havana in the heart of Amsterdam, **Café Cuba** remains a thoroughly enjoyable classic, full of Latin 'gusto'. Come here for the tasty mojitos, old rums or simply for the swinging music. Before you know it, it's suddenly very, very late...
nieuwmarkt 3, phone 020 627 49 19, open sun-thu 13.00-01.00, fri-sat 13.00-03.00, price € 18, tram 1, 2, 4, 5, 9, 13, 16, 17, 24, 25 central station

(22) Inside the oldest city gate of Amsterdam (1488) is the location for bar-restaurant **In de Waag**. Here you can get lunch, have a drink and take dinner, inside next to one metre thick medieval walls and burning candles, or outside on the large terrace.
nieuwmarkt 4, phone 020 422 77 72, open daily 10.00-01.00, price € 34, tram 1, 2, 4, 5, 9, 13, 16, 17, 24, 25 central station

(23) On and around the Nieuwmarkt it's hard to find good but affordable food if you don't happen to fancy Chinese or Thai. Fortunately, however, there is **Eetcafé van Beeren**, with the atmosphere of a 'brown café' and plenty of steaks and fries. Check out the attractive courtyard while you're there.
koningsstraat 54, phone 020 622 23 29, open daily from 17.30, price € 22, tram 1, 2, 4, 5, 9, 13, 16, 17, 24, 25 central station

(25) Not only does **Looks Dining** look hip, it is hip and what's more, it serves really good food ('drunken salmon', 'Baambrugge suckling pig'). The weekly menu varies, but the oysters and entrecote can always be ordered. A special address for special occasions.
binnen bantammerstraat 5-7, phone 020 320 09 49, open daily 19.00-23.00, price € 36, tram 1, 2, 4, 5, 9, 13, 16, 17, 24, 25 central station

IN DE WAAG 22

(27) **Nam Kee** is associated with the book of the same name by writer, Kees van Beijnum, and with famous actress, Katja Schuurman. Nam Kee has good, cheap and authentic Chinese food under disturbingly uninviting fluorescent tube lighting. Whatever you do, don't make the faux pas of asking for peanut sauce or babi panggang (roasted pork).
zeedijk 111, phone 020 624 34 70, open daily 12.00-23.00, price € 12, tram 1, 2, 4, 5, 9, 13, 16, 17, 24, 25 central station

(28) It's unbelievable how quickly they can serve the most delicious Thai dishes at **Snackbar Bird**. This tiny, popular bar is often jam-packed. But if you prefer to take your time, we recommend Bird Thai Restaurant across the street.
zeedijk 72-74, phone snackbar 020 420 62 90, restaurant 020 620 14 42, snackbar open daily 15.00-22.00, restaurant 17.00-22.30, price € 17, tram 1, 2, 4, 5, 9, 13, 16, 17, 24, 25 central station

(29) Wijs & Zonen have been selling their own brand of excellent teas and coffees for ever and a day. The place to experience them is **Hofje van Wijs**, an unexpected slice of romance on the Zeedijk.
zeedijk 43, phone 020 624 04 36, open tue-wed 12.00-19.00, thu-fri 12.00-22.00, sat 10.30-22.00, sun 12.00-19.00, price € 15, tram 1, 2, 4, 5, 9, 13, 16, 17, 24, 25 central station

(30) Experience the atmosphere of old Amsterdam in bar In **'t Aepjen** (At the monkeys). This is where the Dutch saying 'having stayed at the monkeys' originated in the 15th century: if guests couldn't pay the bill, the owner asked them to pay with monekys that sailors had brought back from their travels. The animals were always covered in fleas, so if people saw a person on the Zeedijk frantically scratching himself, they'd say 'he's stayed at the monkeys'.
zeedijk 1, phone 020 626 84 01, open mon-thu, sun 15.00-01.00, fri-sat 15.00-03.00, price € 3, tram 1, 2, 4, 5, 9, 13, 16, 17, 24, 25 central station

(34) **Brasserie Harkema** surprises with its large open space, high ceilings and modern décor, and the enormous wine rack and rainbow-striped wall really catch the eye. It's a good place for a quick bite before taking in a show at one of the near-by theatres.
nes 67, phone 020 428 22 22, open daily 11.00-01.00, price € 23, tram 4, 9, 16, 24, 25 rokin

BRASSERIE HARKEMA

Shopping

① Apart from being a nice place to buy a variety of teas, freshly ground coffees or coffee beans, **Geels & Co** is also a (very small) museum, where you can learn all about tea and coffee. Let yourself be seduced by the heavenly aromas and flavours.
warmoestraat 67, phone 020 624 06 83, open mon-sat 11.00-17.00, sun 13.00-17.00, tram 1, 2, 4, 5, 9, 13, 16, 17, 24, 25 central station

⑥ The building alone is reason enough to visit **Magna Plaza**. If you like shopping, this is a place where you can really let rip, with four floors of stylish shops selling brands such as Replay, Laundry Industry, Mango and Dr. Adams.
nieuwezijds voorburgwal 182, phone 020 626 91 99, open mon 11.00-19.00, tue, wed, fri, sat 10.00-19.00, thu 10.00-21.00, sun 12.00-19.00, tram 1, 2, 5, 6, 13, 17 dam

⑦ If you're looking for something special for your feet, make your way to **Betsy Palmer**. This wonderful shop with its bright red walls is simply packed with cool footwear. Besides their own brand, Betsy Palmer sell Tod's, Blom, Uggs and other hip brands.
rokin 9-15, phone 020 422 10 40, open mon-fri 10.30-18.30, sat 10.00-18.00, sun 13.00-18.00, tram 4, 9, 16, 24, 25 dam

⑫ Dutch Design has conquered the world and **Droog Design** has played an important role in the conquest. In the shop/showroom you'll come face to face with world-famous Dutch design in pieces both large and small.
staalstraat 7b, phone 523 50 59, www.droogdesign.nl, open tue-sat 12.00-18.00, sun 12.00-17.00, tram 4, 9, 16, 24, 25 muntplein

⑬ Dangerously delicious chocolates, or rather 'bomboni', are to be found at **Puccini**. From the traditional bomboni with caramel or marzipan to the out-of-the-ordinary lemongrass or pepper, be warned: these products are highly addictive!
staalstraat 17, phone 020 626 54 74, open mon 12.00-18.00, tue-sat 09.00-18.00, sun 12.00-18.00, tram 4, 9, 16, 24, 25 muntplein

Koffiebranderij
Specialiteit in
Koffie en Thee
GEELS & CO. B.V.
1

MAGNA PLAZA
6

16
SEVE

14

(14) Right behind the building containing the Stadshuis (city hall) and Muziektheater (concert hall) is **Waterlooplein** (Waterloo Square) market, with no less than three hundred stalls of mainly second-hand goods. 'If you can't buy it here, it doesn't exist' is a phrase you often hear here. Prices are not as low as they were, but Waterlooplein market is still fun.
waterlooplein, open mon-sat 10.00-17.00, tram 9, 14 waterlooplein

(16) **Seventyfive** is the address for limited editions of different brands of gym shoes and trainers. Models are often on sale here a few months earlier than elsewhere. And keep an eye out for the sales.
nieuwe hoogstraat 24, phone 020 626 46 11, open mon 12.00-18.00, tue-fri 10.00-18.00, sat 10.00-17.00, sun 13.00-17.00, tram 4, 9, 16, 24, 25 dam

(17) All that glitters is not gold at **Biba**. Here you can buy jewellery by famous designers like Otazu, Gem Kingdom, Vivienne Westwood, J.P.G. Scooter, John Hardy and many others. They also have exclusive jewellery for men.
nieuwe hoogstraat 26, phone 020 330 57 21, open mon 13.00-18.00, tue-sat 11.00-18.00, sun 13.00-17.00, tram 4, 9, 16, 24, 25 dam

(18) At **Zipper** you can browse between shelves and baskets full of second-hand clothes: blouses from the 50's and 60's, shiny jackets, bell-bottom trousers, miniskirts, belts, boots and much, much more.
nieuwe hoogstraat 10, phone 020 627 03 53, open mon-wed, fri-sat 11.00-18.00, thu 11.00-21.00, sun 13.00-17.00, tram 4, 9, 16, 24, 25 dam

(19) Located in a beautiful building, **Puck** is a romantic little shop offering pretty second-hand dresses, blouses, hats, jewellery and other accessories. There's also a small collection of new clothes for young and old alike.
nieuwe hoogstraat 1, phone 020 625 42 01, open mon-fri 11.00-18.00, sat 11.00-17.00, tram 4, 9, 16, 24, 25 dam

Fun things to do

(24) Stroll along the city's lesser-known canals and backwaters. Everyone knows about Herengracht and Prinsengracht, but the neighbourhood round the **Recht Boomssloot, Krom Boomssloot** and **Oudeschans** may well be amongst the prettiest in all Amsterdam. Don't miss the Montelbaanstoren on Oude Schans, an old defence tower dating from 1516. Why's it called that? Nobody knows...
krom boomssloot, recht boomssloot, oude schans, tram 4, 9, 16, 24, 25 dam

(31) Take a walk through the **red-light district**. Stroll along Oudezijds Achterburgwal and Oudezijds Voorburgwal. Don't miss Trompettersteeg, Amsterdam's narrowest street, and Casa Rosso. From the Stoofbrug bridge, you get a nice view of the red-light district and all the coloured lights at night.
oudezijds voorburgwal and oudezijds achterburgwal, tram 1, 2, 4, 5, 9, 13, 16, 17, 24, 25 central station

(35) A visit to the new **Comedy Theater** in de Nes is a must. This lovely little theatre for cabaret and stand-up comedy has had a rapid rise to fame. Big, small and sometimes rather unlikely names take to the stage here. There's even a special children's cabaret.
nes 110, phone 020 422 27 77, www.comedytheater.nl, admission varies, tram 9, 14, 16, 24, 25 rokin

24

24

comedy
theater
in de
Nes
COMEDY THEATER
35

24

City centre

WALK 1

Walk from Central Station in the direction of Dam Square. Turn left before the Beurs van Berlage and take the second street right, Warmoesstraat 1 2 and continue down it to Dam Square 3 4 5 6. Exit Dam Square via Rokin 7 and take a left into Langebrugsteeg. Enter the alley Gebed Zonder End 8 or follow Grimburgwal until you reach Oudemanhuispoort 9. Go right through the gate and continue on Nieuwe Doelenstraat 10 11, or cross the bridge to Staalstraat 12 13. Keep on till Waterlooplein 14. Enter Jodenbreestraat to visit the Rembrandthuis 15 and on Sint Antoniebreestraat go right into Nieuwe Hoogstraat 16 17 18 19. When you reach the water at Kloveniersburgwal, take a right turn towards Nieuwmarkt 20 21 22. Cross Nieuwmarkt towards Geldersekade and go right into Koningsstraat 23. Check out Kromboomsloot 24 or turn left towards Oude Waal. Via Binnenbantammerstraat 25 and Geldersekade backtrack to Nieuwmarkt. Go straight across the square and turn right into Zeedijk, where the Buddhist temple 26 welcomes your arrival in Chinatown. Zeedijk feels like a world of its own with its authentic Asian shops and restaurants, including the famous Nam Kee 27 and snackbar Bird 28. However, not everything here is Oriental: the Hofje van Wijs 29 for example, couldn't be more Dutch. At the top of Zeedijk you'll come across one of the two remaining wooden houses in Amsterdam 30. Go left into Sint Olofspoort and left again onto Oudezijds Voorburgwal. You're now in the red-light district 31. In the canal house at number 46 there is said to be a hidden pearl 32. A little further along is the Oude Kerk 33. If you'd like to explore the red-light district some more, keep going along Oudezijds Voorburgwal and Oudezijds Achterburgwal. Complete your walk by turning right on Oudezijds Voorburgwal into Damstraat and then left onto Nes 34 35.

Jordaan

In the Jordaan you will find plenty of nice little shops, typical Dutch 'brown' cafés and restaurants. The area has a real buzz about it, but is also very pretty with lean/narrow canals, streets and secluded 'hofjes' (courtyards). The Westerkerk rises high above the houses while on the Prinsengracht is the house in which Anne Frank wrote her famous wartime diary. The Brouwersgracht may well be the most romantic part of all Amsterdam. And you'll find no trams or buses and hardly any cars here. The Jordaan feels a bit like a village nestled in the heart of Amsterdam.

Nowadays you rarely come across a real 'Jordaanian' here, with their distinctive flat local accent. Most moved out to Almere or Purmerend in the 1970s, since when the house prices have gone up considerably and the Jordaan.

6x what not to miss!

Noordermarkt

Visit the Saturday organic market.

Anne Frank Huis

Visit the house where Anne Frank wrote her diary.

Papeneiland

Drink a beer in café Papeneiland.

Karthuizerhofje

Wander the small streets and visit a 'hofje'.

Kat in de Wijngaert

Eat a toasted sandwich.

The Movies

Watch a movie at The Movies.

- **Places of interest**
- **Shopping**
- **Food & drinks**
- **Fun things to do**

Places of interest

(1) The 85 metre tower of the **Westerkerk** is the symbol of the Jordaan. It was in this 17th century church that Princess (now Queen) Beatrix and Prince Claus married on 10th March 1966. The church is still in use and can be visited for free.
prinsengracht 281, phone 020 624 77 66, www.westerkerk.nl, open mon-fri 11.00-15.00 (april to october), free, tram 13, 14, 17 westermarkt

(2) Visit the hiding place of Anne Frank and her family in the world-famous **Anne Frank House**, where the original diary is on display. If possible, try to visit outside the holiday season and get there as early as you can, as the queues are usually (very) long. You can now also buy your ticket for the Anne Frank House online, thus avoiding the long queues.
prinsengracht 267, phone 020 556 71 00, www.annefrankhuis.nl, september through march 09.00-19.00, april through june 09.00-21.00, july and august 09.00-22.00, admission adults € 8, children 10-17 year € 4, younger € 0.50, tram 13,14, 17 westermarkt

(16) The listed **Noorderkerk** was built in the early 17th century for residents of the northern part of the Jordaan as the Westerkerk was too far away. One of the annexes of the church, which is now used by the Dutch Reformed Church, houses the City of Amsterdam Archaeology Department.
noordermarkt 44, open mon & thu-sat 11.00-13.00, apr-oct wed 11.00-15.00 & sun 12.00-17.30, free, tram 13, 14, 17 westermarkt

SPANJER
Café
LELIEGRACHT 60
VAN TWIST
3

6

Bier
10

Places to eat & drink

(3) **Spanjer & Van Twist** is a cosy restaurant serving good but affordable food for lunch and dinner. There's a large reading table and during the summer the terrace overlooking the canal is a popular spot.
leliegracht 60, phone 020 639 01 09, open mon-fri 10.00-00.00, sat-sun 10.00-01.00, price € 21, tram 13, 14, 17 westermarkt

(4) **De Reiger** is a pleasant 'eetcafé' (pub restaurant) where you can get a beer at the bar before having dinner. On the menu you'll find simple dishes such as steak with baked potatoes and salad. The atmosphere is relaxed and the staff friendly.
nieuwe leliestraat 34, phone 020 624 74 26, open mon-sat 11.00-01.00, sun 11.00-0.00, price € 26, tram 13, 14, 17 westermarkt

(5) You're in the real Jordaan when you're in **Eetcafé Jur**. Not a trendy lounge or wine bar, just a one-off pleasant bar where you can get good food, ranging from cheese fondue to Saté Jur with Jur-fries. The building used to be the home of long-dead Dutch comedian, Wim Sonneveld, but nowadays, when it's getting late and lively, you're more likely to hear the songs of André Hazes coming through the speakers...
egelantiersgracht 72-74, telephone 020 423 4287, www.eetcafejur.com, open 12.00-23.00, price € 20, tram 13, 14, 17 westermarkt

(6) The little terrace on the canal is one of the real plus points of **Café 't Smalle**. It's an ideal spot for summer lunch watching the canal traffic glide by. This narrow building is decorated as one would expect of a typical 'brown cafés. The house wine is considered one of the very best in town.
egelantiersgracht 12, phone 020 623 96 17, open sun-thu 10.00-01.00, fri-sat 10.00-02.00, price € 6, tram 13, 14, 17 westermarkt

(7) Don't ask for syrup at **Japanese Pancakes World**. Japanese pancakes, or 'okonomiyaki', have very little to do with the trusted Dutch pancake. You can choose from three types of pancakes with a large variety of fillings, from slices of beef with spring onion to shrimps and shiitake. Delicious and different.
tweede egelantiersdwarsstraat 24a, phone 020 320 44 47, open tue-sun 12.00-22.00, price € 14, tram 13, 14, 17 westermarkt

(10) The large, open space of trattoria **Cinema Paradiso** is always packed with hip people. The food is Italian: antipasti, bruschetta, pizza or pasta, and a glass of the famous Scroppino for dessert. It's not possible to book a table in advance, but there is a nice bar to have a drink while you wait!
westerstraat 186, phone 020 623 73 44, open tue-sun 18.00-23.00, price € 25, tram 13, 14, 17 westermarkt

(12) **Kat in de Wijngaert** is well-known as the favourite bar of Dutch filmmaker Eddy Terstall ('Simon', 'Hufters & Hofdames') and many of his regular cast. But even if you've never heard of Eddy, you've still come to the right place, as this is where they serve the best toasted sandwich in town, according to Amsterdam's newspaper Het Parool. You'll find that typical Jordaanian atmosphere and, as the bar name suggests, a very sweet cat.
lindengracht 160, phone 020 622 45 54, open sun-thu 10.00-01.00, fri-sat 10.00-2.00, price € 2, tram 13, 14, 17 westermarkt

(13) A night in tapas bar **Duende** never disappoints, unless you have a problem ordering your dinner at the bar yourself. The tapas are tasty and affordable, and there's a nice laidback atmosphere. There are no reservations.
lindengracht 62, phone 020 420 66 92, open sun-thu 16.00-01.00, fri-sat 16.00-03.00, price € 23, tram 13, 14, 17 westermarkt

(15) At **Eetcafé Koevoet** you'll be served in a typical Amsterdam mezzanine. Intimate, romantic and a tad old-fashioned, this restaurant serves delicious food such as grilled catfish skewer, marinated veal escalope and surprisingly exciting pastas. For dessert try parfait of Bokkenpootjes ('goat hooves') or the chocolate mousse.
lindenstraat 17, phone 020 624 08 46, open thu-sun 18.00-01.00, price € 28, tram 13, 14, 17 westermarkt

(18) **De Winkel** in the heart of the Jordaan, is for many a favourite spot for something to a bite and a drink. The apple pie is heavenly. During the summer, the long wooden tables outside are popular. Grab a seat, order a glass of rosé and curiously you suddenly find you've lost the need to be somewhere else.
noordermarkt 43, phone 020 623 02 23, open mon-thu 08.00-00.00, fri-sat 08.00-03.00, price € 20, tram 13, 14, 17 westermarkt

LINDENGRACHT 162
Duende
CAFE
13

18

(19) **Proust** can get really busy, especially on Friday afternoons. This popular, student-style place is great not just for a drink, but also a good dinner.
noordermarkt 5, phone 020 623 91 45, open tue-thu 12.00-01.00, fri 12.00-03.00, sat 10.00-3.00, sun 12.00-1.00, price € 19, tram 13, 14, 17 westermarkt

(20) One of the most authentic 'brown cafés' in Amsterdam is **Papeneiland**. The small pub set in a marvellous historic building is one of the oldest in town. Delft Blue tiles, eggs on the counter and a woodstove. There's no music, so make sure you have enough to talk about.
prinsengracht 2, phone 020 624 19 89, open mon 09.00-01.00, tue-thu 10.00-01.00, fri 10.00-2.00, sat 09.00-02.00, sun 12.00-01.00, price € 2.50, tram 13, 14, 17 westermarkt

(21) **Café Tabac** is located in an extremely beautiful corner of Amsterdam. The kind of neighbourhood celebrated in Amsterdam folk songs. Settle outside on one of the cushions or go inside and enjoy a drink or choose from the basic but tasty mainly Oriental cuisine.
brouwersgracht 101, phone 020 622 44 13, open mon 11.00-01.00, tue-thu 16.00-01.00, fri 16.00-03.00, sat 11.00-03.00, sun 11.00-01.00, price € 2.50, tram 13, 14, 17 westermarkt

(31) For an uncomplicated fun night out, try dinner at **De Eetkamer van de Jordaan** (The Jordaan dining room). The frequently changing menu has delicious dishes such as grilled tuna steak, tournedos (beef) stroganoff and a Parma ham salad.
westerstraat 76, phone 020 625 07 46, open daily 17.30-01.00, price € 32, tram 13, 14, 17 westermarkt

(32) For those seeking an authentic 'Mokkum' (Amsterdam) night out hit **Café Nol**. Absorb the atmosphere and the booze in this kitschy, typical Jordaan bar where locals, students and other half-cut night owls join sing-along to André Hazes, Willy Alberti and other local heroes of the typical Amsterdam tear-jerker folk songs. Get there after midnight and make sure you're not completely sober.
westerstraat 109, phone 020 624 53 80, open sun-mon 21.00-3.00, wed-thu 21.00-03.00, fri-sat 21.00-04.00, price € 3, tram 13, 14, 17 westermarkt

Eetkamer o/d Jordaa
31

NOL
Café Nol
32

22

14

Shopping

(8) A visit to **De Kleedkamer** can be rewarded with the most fantastic bargains: Next-to-new Prada shoes, second-hand Diesel jeans and pretty dresses that have been worn just once. The shop window is filled with beautiful jewellery and stylish hats. Unfortunately for shopaholic men, they only sell women's clothing.
tweede egelantiersdwarsstraat 8, phone 020 421 08 38, open mon & wed-sat 11.00-18.00, tram 13, 14, 17 westermarkt

(9) Looking for a trendy vintage sweater or a pair of 60's style trousers? You'll find them in **Moriaan**, a shop with loads of original, easy-to-wear second-hand clothing.
tweede anjeliersdwarsstraat 19, phone 020 620 47 98, open mon-sat 11.00-18.00, tram 13, 14, 17 westermarkt

(14) **Donald Jongejans** has been getting noticed for its wide assortment of fantastic spectacle frames dating from 1800 up to the present day. More original than your average optician and with very affordable prices.
noorderkerkstraat 18, phone 020 624 68 88, open mon, fri, sat 11.00-16.00, tram 13, 14, 17 westermarkt

(22) The **Dot-shop** surprises with its contemporary colour combinations and prints on lamp shades, pillows and curtains, all of which have been personally designed. An ideal place to visit if you're planning to pimp up your interior.
haarlemmerdijk 71, phone 020 612 40 30, open tue-wed, fri 10.00-18.00, thu 10.00-21.00, sat 10.00-17.00, tram 3 haarlemmerplein

(23) Welcome to this candy paradise. In the living candy factory **Papa Bubble**, where all your candy dreams come true, they create your sweets before your eyes, including the most bizarre-shaped lollipops and sweets.
haarlemmerdijk 70, phone 020 626 2662, open mon 12.00-18.00, tue-sat 10.00-18.00, tram 3 haarlemmerplein

(24) Visit **Cellarrich** if you're wanting a trendy purse or wallet. Apart from their own collection of bags of washable suede, cow's hide and leather, they also sell other brands of bags. The table in the middle of the shop displays beautiful jewellery and accessories.
haarlemmerdijk 98, phone 020 626 55 26, open mon 13.00-18.00, tue-fri 11.00-18.00, sat 11.00-17.00, tram 3 haarlemmerdijk

(25) The best art house movies are not generally to be found in your average DVD-shop. You may however find them in the small, and pleasingly disorganised **Silver Screen**. The place for that DVD you've been looking for for years, unique film posters and other memorabilia. A visit to this shop is a must for every film fanatic.
haarlemmerdijk 94, phone 020 638 13 41, open tue-sat 13.00-18.00, tram 3 haarlemmerplein

(26) **Vivian Hann's shop** has a style and atmosphere all its own. The focus is on aesthetics, simplicity and quality. Here you can find Chinaware from Dibbern, Rosenthal and Royal Kopenhagen; German pottery from Pott; Japanese porcelain; table linen from Margit Seland; and many more beautiful things besides.
haarlemmerdijk 102, phone 06 22 049 465, open wed-fri 11.00-17.30, sat 10.30-17.00, tram 3 haarlemmerplein

(27) Que bella! **Ramona** is all about the newest Italian shoes. This cute little corner shop offers a limited but exquisite selection of Milanese top quality stuff, as well as beautiful bags and accessories.
haarlemmerdijk 124, phone 020 625 18 70, open mon 13.00-18.00, tue-fri 10.00-18.00, sat 10.00-17.30, tram 3 haarlemmerplein

(28) At **Teuntje**, the grown-ups can browse while the children play. Teuntje sells children's clothing from (European) sizes 50 to 140, shoes up to size 30, strollers from Bugaboo and Easy Walker, and lots of great toys.
haarlemmerdijk 132, phone 020 625 34 32, open mon 13.00-18.00, tue-fri 10.00-18.00, sat 10.00-17.00, tram 3 haarlemmerplein

TEUNTJE (28)

ANNO
35
33

34

(30) **XCLSV** is a little reminiscent of Paris' trendiest shop, Colette. In other words, a superb collection of all sorts of creations by Dutch and international designers. This is where you'll find feathered lamps, bear fur coats and mosaic Buddhas. And, for those on a lower budget, amazing bags and bracelets.
eerste boomdwarsstraat 63 (hoek westerstraat), phone 020 330 42 62, open mon 10.00-18.00, wed-fri 11.00-18.00, sat 10.00-18.00, tram 13, 14, 17 westermarkt

(33) At **Anno** you'll find furniture, lamps and other accessories from the 50s through the 80s by well-known and unknown designers alike. The owner has a good eye for beautiful stuff, ranging from art deco to flower power and everything in between.
westerstraat 35, phone 020 421 26 23, open mon 10.00-18.00, wed-fri 11.00-18.00, sat 11.00-17.00, tram 13, 14, 17 westermarkt

(34) Apart from clothing made by **Margriet Nannings** herself, this women's clothing shop also sells labels such as Paul Smith, Isabelle Marant and Girbeaud. In the men's clothing shop you'll find Comme des Garçons, Paul Smith again, John Richmond and Victor Victoria. In the outlet store on Herenstraat 24, you can buy old collections from both shops.
herenstraat 8 & 15 & 24, phone 020 420 20 97, open mon 13.00-18.00, tue-wed & fri-sat 10.30-18.00, thu 10.30-20.00, tram 13, 14, 17 westermarkt

(35) **Outras Coisas** is really too small for everything the owner wants to display. The shop is literally stuffed with original interior decorations and other accessories, from bags to pottery. The sort of shop where you'd buy everything if you could.
herenstraat 31, phone 020 625 72 81, open sun-mon 13.00-17.00, tue-sat 10.00-18.00, tram 13, 14, 17 westermarkt

16 NOORDERMARKT

Fun things to do

(11) The Jordaan is well known for its numerous 'hofjes' (courtyards). You need to know where they are, because they tend to be hidden away behind inconspicuous doors or entrance gates. But take a peek behind one of those doors and you enter a completely different world in the form of a green and pleasant oasis of peacefulness. The **Karthuizerhofje** is one such and dates back to 1650, when it was built for poor widows. Today a housing corporation lets the houses as private residential homes.
karthuizerstraat 21-131, tram 13, 14, 17 westermarkt

(17) The best places to experience the real Jordaan atmosphere are the markets. Every Saturday, there is an organic farmer's market at the **Noordermarkt**. On the same square you'll also find some stalls selling second-hand furniture and antiques. The market on the Lindengracht offers fish, meat, vegetables, clothing and fabrics. The lapjesmarkt (fabric market), every Monday morning on the Noordermarkt, is also fun.
noordermarkt, sat farmer's market 9.00-16.00, mon fabric-market 9.00-12.00, tram 13, 14, 17 westermarkt

(29) The oldest cinema in Amsterdam is not the famous Tuschinski but **The Movies**, which dates back to 1912. The beautiful art deco interior and comfortable seats make The Movies a stylish place to catch what are usually cult or better quality films.
haarlemmerdijk 161, phone 020 638 60 16 (reservations after 16.30), www.themovies.nl, admission adults € 8.50-9, children € 7, tram 3 haarlemmerplein

Jordaan

WALK 2

Walk from the Westerkerk 1 via Prinsengracht into the Jordaan. Very soon you will pass the Anne Frank House 2. Either cross the bridge and turn right for a cup of coffee at Spanjer & Van Twist 3 or cross the bridge on the left, keep left and then turn right towards the left side of the Egelantiersgracht. Via Eerste Leliedwarsstraat enter the Nieuwe Leliestraat 4. Turn right again and walk back to the Egelantiersgracht 5. Continue until you reach the terrace of 't Smalle 6 or turn left into Tweede Egelantiersdwarsstraat 7 8 and Tweede Anjeliersdwarsstraat 9. Here you'll find some more great shops. Cross the picturesque Westerstraat (you'll return here later on in your walk), where you'll notice Cinema Paradiso 10. Enter Tichelstraat and then turn right into Karthuizerstraat, where a 'hofje' is hidden halfway up the street 11. Turn left on Tweede Lindendwarsstraat and right onto Lindengracht, where you can eat the best toasted sandwiches in town 12 and fantastic tapas 13. Turn right into the Noorderkerkstraat 14. A little bit down on the right on Lindenstraat you'll find a nice little restaurant 15. Continue on this street towards Noordermarkt 16 17. You can take lunch (including great apple pie!) at De Winkel 18 at the corner of Noordermarkt and Westerstraat, or at one of the many other cafes located on the square 19. Walk north now along Prinsengracht towards the bridge opposite Papeneiland 20. From both here and across the water 21 you have an amazing view of the canal. From Brouwersgracht turn left and walk via Korte Prinsengracht to Haarlemmerdijk to indulge in some great shopping therapy 22 23 24 25 26 27 28. Check out The Movies 29 for the beautiful art deco interior. Turn left onto the Haarlemmerplein and then, via Nieuwe Wagenstraat, left onto Brouwersgracht. Now turn right onto the bridge over the Palmgracht and left onto Palmdwarsstraat. Continue down this street and for more shops and great restaurants turn right into Westerstraat 30 31 32 33. Back on track, take Violettenstraat and at the end, turn left into Anjeliersstraat, then right at Prinsengracht, where you cross the bridge. Should you still feel the urge for more shopping, continue straight onto Prinsenstraat and Herenstraat 34 35. This is also a great place to finish with a drink.

3

In the Negen Straatjes it's still possible to take your time while shopping without people constantly getting under your feet - how different from the crowds on Kalverstraat! The area offers a wide range of small boutiques, with everything from clothes and shoes shops, second-hand and new, to hip interior design shops, delicatessens, jewellers shops and hairdressers, with new 'hot spots' emerging on a regular basis. And even if you're not a big one for shopping, this is still a very pleasant area for a walk, as you stroll the streets, feasting your eyes on the beautiful canal views and historic buildings.

6x what not to miss!

Metz & Co

Enjoy the views in the luxurious warehouse.

Pancakes!

Indulge in the special pancakes.

Kitsch Kitchen

Be inspired at Kitsch Kitchen.

Lady Day

Surprise yourself with an antique discovery.

De Looier

Look for unique interior decorations.

De Kaaskamer

Buy some truly pungent cheese.

- Places of interest
- Shopping
- Food & drinks
- Fun things to do

Places of interest

(1) It's not the Bijenkorf on Dam Square, but **Metz & Co** that is Amsterdam's most luxurious department store. That is, if you're looking for expensive furniture or designer clothing. Top notch (literally) is the bar restaurant on the top floor. Designed by world famous Dutch architect and furniture designer Gerrit Rietveld, it offers a wonderful view of the city. And serves a delicious afternoon tea.
leidsestraat 34-36, phone 020 520 72 20, open 10.00-18.00, sat 10.00-17.00, price € 15, tram 1, 2, 5 herengracht

(2) Don't forget to visit **Reguliersdwarsstraat**. This street is the famous heart of gay Amsterdam. Especially during the Amsterdam Pride Festival, the gay and the straight come together here to party round the various stages. There are several good restaurants in this street as well as some rather nice shops.
tram 1, 2, 5 koningsplein

(17) Statues of the icons of the local Jordaan folksong are to be found on **Johnny Jordaanplein**, which is technically a part of Elandsgracht. See the statues of famous Amsterdam folk singers such as Tante ('Aunty') Leen, Manke (lame) Nelis and Johnny Meijer himself and connect with the real Amsterdam.
tram 7, 10 elandsgracht

Places to eat & drink

(5) It's debatable whether the **Vlaams Friteshuis** ('Flemish Chip shop') is the best snack bar in town, but judging from the crowds drawn to the freshly cut and fried fries, many locals think so. The chips come with mayonnaise (of course), but also superior Belgian sauces such as americaine, andalouse, tartare and lemon mayonnaise.
voetboogstraat 33, phone 020 624 6075, open daily 12.00-18.00, price € 2.75, tram 1, 2, 5 spui

(7) Visit **Lef** for a delicious salad or well-filled sandwich in this no-nonsense lunchroom. They also do toasties and smoothies. The place may be small, but the portions are generous.
wijde heisteeg 1, phone 020 620 57 68, open mon & wed-sun 09.00-17.00, price € 9, tram 1, 2, 5 spui

(9) **Goodies** is perfect for a quick, reasonably priced pasta or salad and is also open for lunch. The trendy but cosy interior has white wooden tables and benches. In the summer there's a small terrace.
huidenstraat 9, phone 020 625 61 22, open mon-thu 12.00-01.00, fri 12.00-03.00, sat 11.00-03.00, sun 12.00-01.00, price € 22, tram 1, 2, 5 spui

(15) Order a few small Italian snacks and a drink, and you've got yourself a perfect night at **Festina Lente**. Inside you can relax on big sofas or play a board game. Outside, you can enjoy a warm summer's night on the benches by the canal.
looiersgracht 40b, phone 020 638 14 12, open mon-thu 10.30-01.00, fri-sat 10.30-03.00, sun 12.00-01.00, price € 19, tram 7, 10 elandsgracht

(18) There's both nostalgia and new discoveries to be found at **Pancakes!** This place is a veritable ode to the world of pancakes. A pancake paradise loved by young and old alike. You can order a traditional Dutch bacon pancake, and if you're brave enough they'll even add banana or chilli peppers. In this restaurant with its Dutch interior, the menu also offers Russian blini, French crepes, Surinamese roti and tortillas.
berenstraat 38, phone 020 528 97 97, open daily 10.00-19.00, price € 12, www.pancakesamsterdam.nl, tram 1, 2, 5 spui

22

31
Nihon Ryouri

(20) **Nielsen** is a popular breakfast and lunch bar. Start your day here with a freshly made smoothie, a bagel or an omelette. For lunch, a club sandwich or a salad are good choices. But do make sure you're not in a hurry…
berenstraat 19, phone 020 330 60 06, open tue-thu 08.00-16.00, fri 08.00-17.00, sat 08.00-18.00, sun 09.00-17.00, price € 14, tram 1, 2, 5 spui

(22) **Brix** is a nice restaurant that serves snacks from across the globe. It's nicely decorated with dark mirrors and an exposed brick wall and there are jamming sessions held here every Friday night.
wolvenstraat 16, phone 020 639 03 51, open mon-thu 16.00-01.00, fri 16.00 03.00, sat 14.00-03.00, sun 14.00-01.00, price € 22, tram 1, 2, 5 spui

(27) A bit weird, but a good place all the same, **Schuim** is one of the classier bars and meeting-up spots in town. This slightly 'arty' place has got artists to contribute to its interior design. Great for a simple meal or drink, or a dance and flirt at the weekend!
spuistraat 189, phone 020 638 93 57, open sun-thu 11.00-01.00, fri-sat 11.00-03.00 price € 17, tram 1, 2, 5, 13, 17 dam

(30) **Van Harte** is a popular restaurant where you can enjoy a meal and a drink in a very friendly atmosphere. Also open for lunch, the middle of the restaurant is a bar and the colourful wallpaper brings an instant smile to your face.
hartenstraat 24, phone 020 625 85 00, open daily 11.00-23.00, price € 34, tram 1, 2, 5, 13, 14, 17 dam

(31) If you enjoy authentic Japanese cuisine, **Kagetsu** is exceptionally good. The Chicken Teriyaki, California hand rolls and noodles are mouth-watering. There are red chopsticks for the ladies and black ones for the gentlemen. Note: cash payment only!
hartenstraat 17, phone 020 427 38 28, open tue-sun 17.00-22.30, price € 20, tram 1, 2, 5, 13, 14, 17 dam

Shopping

(3) People have been known to lose hours in **Selexyz Scheltema**. For years, this has been renowned as Amsterdam's largest bookshop. There are occasional signings and there's an in-house coffee and bagel shop. Five floors and 125,000 book titles.
koningsplein 20, phone 523 14 11, open mon 12.00-18.00, tue-wed & fri-sat 10.00-18.00, thu 10.00-21.00, sun 12.00-18.00, tram 1, 2, 5 koningsplein

(8) Onitsuka what? **Onitsuka Tiger** are super trendy Japanese trainers. The brand was originally established to make Japanese youngsters more self-confident. Here you'll find this exciting brand's latest unique runners and even jeans.
herengracht 356, on the corner of huidenstraat, phone 020 528 61 83, open mon 13.00-18.00, tue-sat 10.00-18.00, tram 1, 2, 5 herengracht

(10) Design your own jewellery. At **Beadies** you'll find an abundance of pretty beads, pendants and other shiny stuff. You can also buy ready-made earrings, bracelets and necklaces.
huidenstraat 6, phone 020 428 51 61, open mon-wed & fri-sat 10.30-18.00, thu 10.30-21.00, tram 1, 2, 5 spui

(11) Clothing by Dries Van Noten, Ann Demeulemeester, Dirk Bikkembergs and other top Belgian fashion designers are on offer at **Van Ravenstein**. Also check out the bargain basement, where you can sometimes find something special from old collections.
keizersgracht 359, phone 020 639 00 67, open mon 13.00-18.00, tue-wed & fri 11.00-18.00, thu 11.00-19.00, sat 10.30-17.30, tram 1, 2, 5 spui

(12) Even though there's more on offer here, one famous designer stands out at the two corner shops of **Local Service**: Paul Smith. His sleek suits, unmistakable stripes and beautiful accessories are well worth the visit.
keizersgracht 400hs & 402, phone 020 626 8 40, open mon 12.00-18.00, tue-wed & fri-sat 10.00-18.00, thu 10.00-21.00, sun 10.00-17.00, tram 1, 2, 5 spui

kralen, sieraden en accessoires
Beadies
10

0,35
3,95
10

(13) **De Kaaskamer** ('cheese chamber') has cheeses drenched in calvados, wrapped in wine leaves and other intriguing creations. Cheese lovers come to this powerfully aromatic shop for its unbelievable selection of cheeses from Holland, obscure French mountain regions and undiscovered Italian islands. Complete your picnic basket with nuts and tasty sausages.
runstraat 7, phone 020 623 34 83, open mon 12.00-18.00, tue-fri 09.00-18.00, sat 09.00-17.00, sun 12.00-17.00, tram 1, 2, 5 spui

(14) **Shirts and Cappuccino** sells well-cut Italian shirts in line with the latest Milan trends, as well as pullovers, ties, trousers and shoes. Basically, anything but suits. The collection changes regularly and the shirts are imported directly from Italy. Enjoy a great cappuccino while trying on the collection.
runstraat 26, phone 020 428 00 93, open mon 13.00-19.00, tue-wed & fri 11.00-19.00, thu 11.00-21.00, sat 11.00-18.00, sun 13.00-17.00, tram 1, 2, 5 spui

(19) **Stout** ('naughty') has lingerie and other playful things for those long, cold winter evenings or sultry summer nights. The collection is for both sexes and includes anything with the potential to raise the body temperature.
berenstraat 9, phone 020 620 16 76, open mon-fri 12.00-19.00, sat 11.00-18.00, sun 13.00-17.00, tram 1, 2, 5 spui

(21) **Parisienne** is an extremely romantic shop selling contemporary Parisian jewellery, as well as frivolous handbags and scarves subtly embroidered with sequins and beads. Bet you'll leave with something nice!
berenstraat 4, phone 020 428 08 34, open mon 13.00-18.00, tue-fri 10.00-18.00, sat 10.00-17.00, sun 12.00-17.00, tram 1, 2, 5 spui

(23) Don't call it a shop, call it a concept; that's what the owners do. **Spoiled/Denimbar** is actually a very trendy clothing shop with all the 'right' brands, where you also get your hair done. There's also the denim bar where you can get advice on the right pair of jeans for you. Brands include: Nudie jeans, Barong Barong, Stella Nova and Tiger of Sweden.
wolvenstraat 19, phone 020 626 38 18, open mon 12.00-18.00, tue-wed & fri-sat 10.00-18.00, thu 10.00-21.00, sun 10.00-17.00, tram 1, 2, 5 spui

(24) One sees more and more Amsterdammers in **Le Coq Sportif** shoes. The French brand has seen a real revival of late and in this flagship shop you can find the complete current collection of les runners, les t-shirts and other sports or street wear. All, naturellement, sporting the famous cockrel logo. *wolvenstraat 14, phone 020 320 40 98, open mon 12.00-18.00, tue-wed & fri-sat 10.00-18.00, thu 10.00-21.00, sun 10.00-17.00, tram 1, 2, 5 spui*

(25) If you're looking for vintage clothing from the 40s and 50s, **Laura Dols** is a must. Browse through flowery dresses, ruched blouses and crocheted tablecloth checks - pure nostalgia! At the back of the shop is the 'Verkleed-komeet' ('costume comet'): a great selection of dress costumes for kids.
wolvenstraat 6-7, phone 020 624 90 66, open mon-sat 11.00-18.00, tram 1, 2, 5 spui

(26) **Urban Picnic** is a shop and a lunchroom in one. In the shop, you'll find sturdy cupboards, tables and chairs, as well as pottery bowls, glassware and colourful plastic picnic tableware. On the menu there are snacks such as Merguez sausages, marinated chicken and various salads, pies and cakes. Small but special.
oude spiegelstraat 4, phone 020 320 88 66, open tue-wed & fri 09.00-18.00, thu 09.00-19.00, sat 10.00-18.00, tram 1, 2, 5 spui

(28) Fashion freaks buy their shoes at **Antonia by Yvette**. Brands include Roberto Botticelli, Roberto Cavalli, Sonia Rykiel, Kop en Staart, Moma, Free-lance and Kickers. Shoes for men and women, plus a small collection of bags.
gasthuismolensteeg 16, 18 & 20, phone 020 320 94 43, open tue-wed & fri-sat 10.00-18.00, thu 10.00-21.00, sun (last sun of every month) 13.00-17.00, tram 1, 2, 5, 13, 14, 17 dam

(29) **Lady Day** buys original vintage clothing from around the world and resells them in this shop. Come here for spotless jackets, including leather jackets, shirts, suits, trousers, cocktail dresses and evening gowns from the 20s through to the 80s. You'll also find a large variety of shoes, pumps and accessories.
hartenstraat 9, phone 020 623 58 20, open mon-wed & fri-sat 11.00-21.00, thu 13.00-18.00, tram 1, 2, 5, 13, 14, 17 dam

PARISIENNE 21

㉝ KITSCH KITCHEN

(32) **Paul Frank's** creations are famous all over the world. Who doesn't know the t-shirts, bags and pullovers with the famous monkey (whose name, incidentally is Julius)? Nowadays Julius has friends like Clancy the giraffe and Sheree the cat.
hartenstraat 23, phone 020 423 25 80, open mon 11.00-18.00, tue-wed & fri-sat 10.00-18.00, thu 10.00-21.00, sun 12.00-18.00, tram 1, 2, 5, 13, 14, 17 dam

(33) It all started with a market stall selling colourful vinyl tablecloths from Mexico. Since when, **Kitsch Kitchen** has grown into a vibrant 'supermercado'. The high, bright-pink wall, the big plastic shopping carts and the numerous original gifts ideas from Mexico and other places around the world have turned this shop into a true shopper's paradise.
rozengracht 8-12, phone 020 622 82 61, open mon-sat 10.00-18.00, tram 13, 14, 17 westermarkt

(34) Lovers of designer furniture can indulge themselves in the three branches of the Kasstoor group along the Rozengracht: **Wonen 2000**, **Wonen 2000 Bed&Bad** (Bed&Bath) and **the Kasstoor** with brands such as Gispen, Kartel, Linteloo and Edra.
rozengracht 202-210, phone 020 521 87 10, open mon-wed & fri 10.00-18.00, thu 10.00-21.00, sat 10.00-17.00, tram 3, 14, 17 rozengracht

(35) Shopping at **SPRMRKT** is a joy for collector's of stuff from the 60s, 70s or 80s. 450 square metres of furniture, bikinis, bathing suits, shirts, ties, scarves and music. They also have art, the occasional car, plus a fashion collection from their own house label.
rozengracht 191-193, phone 020 330 56 01, open tue-sat 10.00-18.00, tram 3, 14, 17 rozengracht

Fun things to do

④ You're confronted with a sea of colours and fragrances when walking through the **Flower market** on Singel. The flowers and plants are displayed on floating barges, a relic from back when this market's merchandise was shipped in from the horticultural regions outside the city.
singelgracht (between koningsplein and muntplein), open mon-fri 09.00-18.30, sat 09.00-17.00, sun 11.00-17.30, free, tram 1, 2, 5 koningsplein

⑥ Every Friday there's a **book market** on Spui. Great for browsing through second-hand and antique books and prints. On Sundays, the Spui transforms into an art market, where artists display their paintings and sculptures.
spui, open fri 09.00-18.00, sun 09.00-17.00, free, tram 1, 2, 5 spui

⑯ **De Looier** is an indoor flea market spread out over some 1750 square metres. Traders here sell an eclectic selection of art, antiques and curiosities. Another great spot for browsing and one of the best places to find that genuinely unique item your home.
elandsgracht 109, phone 020 624 90 38, www.looier.nl, open mon-thu & sat-sun 11.00-17.00, tram 7, 10 elandsgracht

Kunst- & Antiekcentrum
DE
LOOIER

De Negen Straatjes

WALK 3

From the Leidseplein walk down Leidsestraat with its many shops and luxury department store (1) to Koningsplein. Here you can visit the 'pink' street (2) or a book paradise (3). To the right of this square, you'll see countless flower stands (4). Those preferring to get straight on with the shopping, walk from Koningsplein into Heiligeweg, turn left into Voetboogstraat (5) for the most fantastic fries and continue onto Spui, a square with great book shops and the book market (6). Skip the crowded Kalverstraat and instead leave Spui passing the famous Café Hoppe and enter Wijde Heisteeg. This is where the Negen Straatjes start with their many special shops, galleries, lunchtime eateries and restaurants. On Wijde Heisteeg, Lef (7) is a good place for lunch. Keep on into Huidenstraat for shopping or more places to eat and drink (8) (9) (10) (11). Now continue onto Runstraat for more shops (12) (13) (14). For a hint of Amsterdam nostalgia, cross Prinsengracht to Looiersgracht, where you can take a break at Festina Lente (15). Bijna op het eind sla je rechtsaf naar De Looier (16), a large indoor flea and antique market. Walk north via Elandsgracht until you reach Johnny Jordaanplein (17) with its statues of four Amsterdam folksong heroes: Johnny Jordaan, Tante ('Aunty') Leen, Manke (lame) Nelis and Johnny Meijer. You're actually now transgressed into the Jordaan area, so let's move quickly on. Grab a special pancake and continue shopping in Berenstraat (18) (19) (20) (21) and Wolvenstraat (22) (23) (24) (25). Enter Oude Spiegelstraat (Old Mirror Street) for Urban Picnic (26) and then turn left into Spuistraat. Walk, where you can get a well-earned drink (27). Now go left into Paleisstraat and, if you still haven't had enough shopping, take on Gasthuismolensteeg (28) and Hartenstraat (29) (30) (31) (32). Still not satisfied? Cross the bridge and veer right via Prinsengracht and then take the third left into Rozengracht for what are mainly interior design shops (33) (34) (35).

4

Vondelpark, the most popular park in Amsterdam, is the place for picnicking or just hanging out. Especially in the summer months, the park turns into one big open air theatre, abuzz with skaters, joggers, sun worshippers and tourists. To the west of Vondelpark is Overtoom, which has a few very nice interior design shops and a well-hidden treasure in the Hollandsche Manege (Dutch Ménage, or horse riding school). To the east of the park is Oud-Zuid (Old South), one of the wealthiest neighbourhoods in Amsterdam with its mix of old and new money. The area round Cornelis Schuytstraat and Jacob Obrechtstraat has several trendy shops and a choice of restaurants, from the smart to the more homely.

6x what not to miss!

Rijksmuseum

See the masterpieces.

Concertgebouw

Attend a free lunch concert.

P.C. Hooftstraat

Spend money and watch the people.

Hollandsche Manege

Have a look round the Hollandsche Manege.

Vondelpark

Enjoy a picnic in Vondelpark.

Van Gogh Museum

Admire the art in the Van Gogh Museum (on a quiet morning).

- **Places of interest**
- **Shopping**
- **Food & drinks**
- **Fun things to do**

Places of interest

(1) The **Rijksmuseum** is currently undergoing the biggest renovation in the museum's history, due to be finished in 2013, though Rembrandt's 'Nightwatch' and countless other masterpieces from Dutch artists of the Golden Age, such as Johannes Vermeer, Frans Hals and Jan Steen remain on display.
jan luijkenstraat 1, phone 020 674 70 47, www.rijksmuseum.nl, open mon-thu & sat-sun 09.00-18.00, fri 09.00-20.30, admission € 10, tram 2, 5 museumplein

(4) Nowhere in the world you'll find as many pieces by Vincent van Gogh as in the **Van Gogh Museum** itself: over two hundred paintings, five hundred drawings, seven hundred letters plus his collection of Japanese prints.
paulus potterstraat 7, phone 020 570 52 00, www.vangoghmuseum.nl, open mon-thu & sat-sun 10.00-18.00, fri 10.00-22.00, admission € 12.50, tram 3, 5, 12 van baerlestraat

(17) The **Vondelkerk** church is a Neo-Gothic listed building located on the edge of Vondelpark. It was built in 1872 and designed by P.H.J. Cuypers, the architect who also designed Central Station and the Rijskmuseum. At weekends, the main hall of the church can be rented for special events.
vondelstraat 120d, phone 020 689 79 20, www.vondelkerk.nl, tram 1, 3, 12 overtoom/eerste constantijn huygensstraat

(18) Just where you'd never expect to find it is the **Hollandsche Manege** (Dutch Riding School), this stately building from 1882 is based on the Wiener Reitschule. The spacious covered arena with its balustrades and beautiful plaster decorations evokes the grandeur of another age.
vondelstraat 140, phone 020 618 09 42, variable, free, tram 1, 3, 12 overtoom/eerste constantijn huygensstraat

(21) The **Filmmuseum** owns more than a thousand international films. Some of your classier cult movies can be enjoyed in the open air on Saturday nights during July and August. The museum shop sells film photos, posters, scripts and other documents from the end of the 19th century to the present day.
vondelpark 3, phone 020 589 14 00, www.filmmuseum.nl, open daily 09.00-22.00, admission € 7.80, tram 1, 3, 12 overtoom/eerste constantijn huygensstraat

Places to eat & drink

(2) On museumplein (Museum Square) you'll find the **Cobra Café** with its artistic interior and pleasant terrace. From behind the tall windows you have a beautiful view out over the pond and the square. Great club sandwiches, sushi and salads.
hobbemastraat 14, phone 020 470 01 11, open daily 10.00-21.00, price € 28, tram 2, 5 hobbemastraat

(6) Bonjour **Entrecôte et les Dames**... At this very popular restaurant next to the Concert Hall, one really has to go for the tender entrecote served with sauce and fries, though the sole is a good alternative. Go after 8pm, before then it's packed with pre-performance classical music lovers.
van baerlestraat 49, phone 020 679 88 88, open 17.30-23.00, price € 27, tram 2, 5 van baerlestraat

(7) **Bodega Keyzer**, an institute amongst Oud-Zuid old money and business people, has been going through some difficult times in recent years. If it wasn't dodgy owners, then it was lamps falling down. But 'la grande dame' is slowly making her comeback. Real classics, but not cheap, include coquilles St Jacques, tournedos Rossini and fruits de mer. Oud-Zuid at its best.
van baerlestraat 96, phone 020 675 18 66, open mon 11.00-23.00, price € 44, tram 2, 5 van baerlestraat

(10) A lovely terrace in one of the most beautiful streets in Amsterdam. **Toussaint** is an oasis in the middle of Oud-West. Come here for the tasty sandwiches and delicious meals. Across the street, restaurant Bosboom offers a more complex menu.
bosboom toussaintstraat 26, phone 020 685 07 37, open 10.00-23.00, price € 19, tram 1, 3, 7, 12 overtoom/eerste constantijn huygensstraat

(11) Let us tell you a secret. The chef that made Moroccan restaurant Mamouche in the Pijp area famous has started his own place here. It's called **Zina**, the food is heavenly and the décor is pure 1001 nights. Tajines, fresh fruit and delicious spices from the Maghreb are fantastic.
bosboom toussaintstraat 70 bg, phone 020 489 37 07, open 18.00-22.00, price € 35, tram 1, 3, 7, 12 overtoom/eerste constantijn huygensstraat

'T BLAUWE THEEHUIS (22)

㉔ VONDELTUIN

(20) In the atmospheric cafe-restaurant **Vertigo** you can have a drink, lunch or dinner. The large terrace and balcony of the film museum is a favourite spot for Amsterdammers throughout the summer. During the winter, you can sit comfortably inside at wooden tables.
vondelpark 3, phone 020 612 30 21, open daily 10.00-01.00, price € 29, tram 3, 12 van baerlestraat

(22) On the terrace of **'t Blauwe Theehuis** (the Blue Teahouse) you'll meet all sorts of people and when the temperature drops, the jet stoves are switched on. On Friday, Saturday and Sunday evenings there's a dj and dancing is possible.
vondelpark 5, phone 020 662 02 54, open sun-thu 09.00-23.00, fri-sat 09.00-01.00, price € 30, tram 3, 12 van baerlestraat

(23) **Het Groot Melkhuis** (The Big Milk House) has a sizable playground, large terrace from which parents can keep an eye on their children, and a restaurant offering a simple menu including sandwiches and croquet with fries. That muffled pock-pock you can hear comes from neighbouring tennis club, Festina.
vondelpark 2, phone 020 612 96 74, open daily mon-fri 10.00-17.00, sat-sun 10.00-18.00, price € 7, tram 3, 12 van baerlestraat

(24) Why not celebrate your stay in Amsterdam at **Vondeltuin**. When the weather's nice, this is one of the most sociable spots in the park. Just chill out on the recliners or sit at one of the colourful tables. At the bar you can order small dishes such as tapas, pasta, chicken saté, fries and salads.
vondelpark 7, phone 020 664 50 91, open may through october daily 11.00-00.00, price € 13, tram 1 overtoomsesluis

(25) **Sophia** is the name of the latest trendy creation of top chef Ron Blaauw. The tapas, might more accurately be described as exquisite and luxurious nibbles, such as lime and wasabi oysters or rilettes with a sourdough bread-crostini. Or you can just enjoy a cocktail.
sophialaan 55, phone 020 305 27 60, open mon-fri 12.00-01.00, sat-sun 15.00-01.00, price € 34, tram 2 amstelveenseweg

(28) **Affourtit** is a pleasant neighbourhood restaurant with a Mediterranean atmosphere. The international menu offers plenty of choice and changes every two months. During the summer, you can eat outside on the lovely terrace. And should the weather be less good, the heaters on the terrace are switched on. Or they can lend you one of their own Affourtit fleeces...
koninginneweg 209, telephone 020 679 84 17, open sun-thu 17.00-01.00, fri-sat 17.00-02.00, price € 28, tram 2 valeriusplein

(29) **Brasserie Senz** serves delicious dishes and good wines. During the day you can have a tuna sashimi with lemon mayonnaise or a spinach salad with Brie and pommodori. In the evening they serve grilled spring chicken, entrecote or cod fish stew.
emmastraat 29, phone 020 670 83 21, open mon-fri 12.00-22.00, sun 18.00-22.00, price € 33, tram 2 emmastraat

(30) If you're looking for dinner in a cosy brasserie-style restaurant, try **Palma**. The delicious dishes, fine wines and homely atmosphere can turn your visit into a long and pleasant one.
johannes verhulststraat 104, phone 020 379 59 00, open mon-sat 18.00-00.00, price € 35, tram 2 jacob obrechtstraat

(32) **Sal Gorda** is a nice little tapas bar with friendly Spanish waiters. On the menu you'll find well-known tapas favourites like patatas bravas, shrimps in garlic oil, and spicy chicken. Finish your dinner off with a carajillo (espresso) charged with a shot of liqueur.
van breestraat 107a, phone 020 673 08 77, open daily 17.30-00.00, price € 20, tram 2 cornelius schuytstraat/tram 16 valeriusplein

(34) Pub-café **Café de Gruter** has been a popular spot for many years amongst students and local residents. On Friday early evenings in particular, people like to celebrate the start of the weekend here. On other days and in the evening it's the perfect place for a drink and a light bite.
willemsparkweg 73, phone 020 679 62 52, open sun-thu 12.00-01.00, fri-sat 12.00-02.00, tram 2 jacob obrechtstraat

28

29

30

32

Shopping

(8) In the Dutch version of Monopoly, the chic **P.C. Hooftstraat** is one of the most expensive streets on the board. And that reflects real life, with designer shops like Louis Vuitton, DKNY, Dolce & Gabbana, Gucci, Armani and Hugo Boss. You'll come across plenty of expensive cars parked here, as well as local Dutch celebrities and the odd Russian accent. But find out for yourself (and don't forget to call it just 'PC', like the locals).
p.c. hooftstraat, opening hours vary per shop, tram 3, 5, 12 van baerlestraat

(9) **Helden en Boeven** (Heroes and Villains). Great name, great shop. Before moving this upmarket bookshop used to be a well-known landmark on Nieuwmarkt. Specialized in children's book, it also organises film and other (birthday) activities for little ones who just can't face another visit to the zoo.
bosboom toussaintstraat 27, phone 020 427 44 07, open daily 10.00-18.00, mon from 13.00, tram 1, 3, 7, 12 overtoom/eerste constantijn huygensstraat

(12) How can some small shops be so big? **Vleck** offers a wide selection of very special wines from well- and less-known regions, mostly supplied by smaller producers. Bought with love, sold with knowledge. The perfect place to pick up that bottle for your more luxurious picnic in Vondelpark.
eerste helmersstraat 63 hs, phone 020 683 59 80, open mon 14.00-19.00, tue-fri 12.00-19.00, sat 10.00-17.00, tram 1, 3, 7, 12 overtoom/eerste constantijn huygensstraat

(13) Halfway down Overtoom is **Coco-Mat**, a shop specializing in beds and furniture made of natural, ethically produced materials. The basement has an imaginative children's department.
overtoom 89, phone 020 489 29 27, open mon-fri 9.30-18.30, sat 10.00-18.00, sun 12.00-18.00, tram 1, 3, 12 overtoom/eerste constantijn huygensstraat

IMAGINE 26

(14) Every travel enthusiast in Amsterdam is already aware of its existence. **Pied a Terre** is the best, biggest and most beautiful travel bookshop in Amsterdam and far beyond. The building houses a coffee place and browsing area, a large collection of travel guides, globes and trail maps, plus much more to interest the keen traveller. You can spend hours in here.
overtoom 135-137, phone 020 627 44 55, open mon 13.00-18.00, tue-wed & fri 10.00-18.00, thu 10.00-21.00, sat 10.00-17.00, tram 1, 3, 7, 12 overtoom/ eerste constantijn huygensstraat

(15) Nice restaurants, oriental corner shops, fun gift shops and a couple of great bars are all to be found on **Jan Pieter Heijestraat**. It's not quite the Negen Straatjes, but on the upside you'll hardly see any tourists there and the prices reflect that. So you should definitely take a right or left turn every now and then into this street! Incidentally, Jan Pieter Heije was a doctor and a musician, and penned the traditional Dutch children's song 'Zie de maan schijnt door de bomen…' ("See the moon shining through the trees"). Just so you know.
jan pieter heijestraat, tram 1, 7, 17 jan pieter heijestraat

(16) For 50s, 60s and 70s design, go to **Design Overtoom**. This spacious shop is packed with lamps and furniture from mostly Italian designers. A must for anyone into this style.
overtoom 429, phone 020 689 81 50, open mon-sat 10.00-18.00, sun 12.00-18.00, tram 1 jan pieter heijestraat

(26) They call themselves 'the slightly different child shop´ and with good reason. At **Imagine** you'll find unique, handmade presents and original toys, games, clothing and furniture for babies and younger children. The sort of place that can cheer you up.
amstelveenseweg 131, phone 020 670 88 99, open mon 13.00-17.00, tue-fri 10-00-18.00, sat 10.00-17.00, tram 2 zeilstraat

(27) **Casa & Luce** is de moeite waard als je op zoek bent naar een leuk cadeau voor jezelf of iemand anderlunchroom van dezelfde eigenaar.
koninginneweg 220, phone 020 671 65 04, open mon 12.00-18.00, tue-wed & fri 10.00-18.00, thu 10.00-21.00, sat 10.00-17.00, tram 2 zeilstraat

DESIGN OVERTOOM (16)

31 MENNO KROON

(27) **Casa & Luce** is worth a visit if you're looking for a special present, be it for yourself or someone else. Alongside the larger furniture pieces, you'll find trendy lamps, pillows, jewellery and other accessories. And if all that shopping's worn you out, next door is Casa & Cucina, a cheerful lunchroom owned by the same people.
koninginneweg 220, phone 020 671 65 04, open mon 12.00-18.00, tue-wed & fri 10.00-18.00, thu 10.00-21.00, sat 10.00-17.00, tram 2 zeilstraat

(31) **Menno Kroon** creates the most beautiful flower arrangements for every occasion. It's hard to find anything quite like this place anywhere else in the city. The difference between a bouquet and a bunch.
cornelis schuytstraat 11, phone 020 679 19 50, open mon-fri 09.00-18.00, sat 09.00-17.30, tram 2 cornelis schuytstraat

(33) The shoes at **Luuks** are all handmade from the most exquisite leather. Not cheap, but then you're getting something special. Labels include Jeffrey West, Paul Smith, N.D.C., Freelance and (a favourite of Madonna and Victoria Beckham) R.Soles.
jacob obrechtstraat 12, phone 020 670 45 38, open tue-fri 11.30-19.30, sat 11.00-18.00, tram 2 jacob obrechtstraat

(35) **Suit Supply** sells contemporary Italian tailor-made suits, shirts, jackets and trousers. No famous brands, just quality at a reasonable price. A favourite with those starting out on the career ladder who can't quite yet afford 'PC'.
willemsparkweg 37-41, phone 020 471 33 62, open mon 12.00-20.00, tue-wed 11.00-20.00, thu 11.00-21.00, fri 11.00-20.00, sat 10.00-17.00, tram 2 van baerlestraat

Fun things to do

(3) **Museumplein** is looking a little run down of late. It's barely ten years since it was completely overhauled, but over the coming years this special piece of Amsterdam is about to get another major makeover. Nevertheless, this spacious square offers trees, gravel paths, benches and a pond. In winter you can ice-skate on the rink and in summer the square is packed with museum visitors, park footballers and people bathing in the sun with a bottle of wine and a bite.
tram 2, 5 museumplein

(5) **Amsterdam's Concertgebouw** (Concert Hall) is the best attended and one of the very best classical music venues in the world, praised for its perfect acoustics. You'll usually need to make reservations way in advance if you want to go to an evening concert, but there are also very good free lunch concerts every Wednesday afternoon from 12.30 pm till 13.00 pm (come early).
concertgebouwplein 2-6, reservations by phone 020 671 83 45, www.concertgebouw.nl, tram 3, 5, 12 museumplein

(19) It's not difficult to spend hours in **Vondelpark**, especially in summertime. Take a huge quilt and lie out in the sun. If you're looking for a little more action, bring a football or a Frisbee. You can also rent in-line skates at Vondeltuin and take lessons. Look out for the open-air theatre in July and August. Wednesday to Sunday evenings you can enjoy free theatre and dance performances.
constantijn huygenssstraat (various entrances), www.vondelpark.nl, tram 3, 5, 12 van baerlestraat

VONDELPARK 19

Oud-Zuid & Oud West

WALK 4

Welcome to Museumplein. We'll start our walk at the Rijksmuseum (1). On this square you'll also find the Cobra Café (2). Also on Museumplein (3) you'll see an ellipse-shaped building, which is part of the Van Gogh museum (4). Follow the tiled path in the direction of the Concertgebouw (Concert Hall) (5) and walk into Van Baerlestraat for a bite to eat (6) (7). To visit the Van Gogh Museum, you'll need to go via Paulus Potterstraat. If you'd rather go shopping, then walk past the music conservatory towards P.C. Hooftstraat (8). Continue along Van Baerlestraat and cross Overtoom. Keep right on Eerste Constantijn Huygensstraat and enter Tweede Helmersstraat, then turn left into Genestetstraat. You now enter Bosboom Toussaintstraat, known for its children's shops (9) and little restaurants (10) (11). Walk back towards Eerste Constantijn Huygensstraat and then turn left, heading back towards Overtoom. Walk past the wine merchants Vleck (12) and carry on to Coco-Mat (13). Turn right here into Overtoom for the city's most beautiful travel bookshop (14) and carry straight on if you're up for some interior shops (15) (16). Turn into Tweede Constantijn Huygensstraat towards Vondelstraat to visit the beautiful Vondelkerk church (17) and magnificent Hollandsche Manege (18). Now it's time to visit the green lung of the city: Vondelpark (19). Immediately on your left you'll find Vertigo (20) and the Film museum (21). Or turn right if you are looking for a quiet spot to lie down, a glass of rosé at the Blauwe Theehuis (22) or to listen to the sound of kids playing at Het Groot Melkhuis (23). On the most southerly part of the park you come to its nicest spot: Vondeltuin (24). Leave the park from this side and turn left into Amstelveenseweg. Walk down Sophialaan, where you can get something to eat or drink at Sophia (25) or buy something for your kids (26) (27). Or to give your taste buds a treat, walk towards Willemsparkweg (28) and turn right into Emmastraat (29). Go left into Johannes Verhulststraat (30) and past the luxurious shops on Cornelis Schuytstraat (31). Now turn right into Van Breestraat for a Spanish restaurant (32), beyond which you'll discover another chic little shopping street on your left: Jacob Obrechtstraat (33). You can end your walk here at one of this neighbourhood's favourite café's: Gruter (34). Or pop in to buy yourself a new suit... (35).

5

This former working-class area, birthplace of Amsterdam's famous folk singer, Andre Hazes, is currently the trendiest area of the city, comparable to Notting Hill, the Village or the Marais. Alongside the Surinamese food shops, Turkish sewing shops and Islamic butchers, the trendy restaurants are popping up like mushrooms, one after another. The renovated, typically 19th century houses with their long, narrow rooms are much in favour with young working couples and start-up entrepreneurs. Not surprising when you consider that the great atmosphere of Albert Cuyp market and the charm of Sarphati Park are but a few steps away. Students are also drawn to the vibrancy of De Pijp and it is a great area to explore.

6x what not to miss!

Foam

Take in an out-of-the-ordinary photo exhibition.

Amstel

Stroll along the river Amstel admiring the lighted bridges in the evening.

Schiller

Have a drink in the art-deco atmosphere.

Utrechtsestraat

Go shopping for that special outfit, pair of shoes or gadget.

Albert Cuypmarket

Do some cheap-and-cheerful shopping.

Gerard Douplein

Have a drink on one of the terraces on cosy Gerard Douplein.

- **Places of interest**
- **Shopping**
- **Food & drinks**
- **Fun things to do**

Places of interest

(1) **The Munt** (Coin) tower is part of the remains of Reguliers gate, which used to be part of the medieval city wall. The tower was given its name in 1672, when it was no longer possible to transport silver and gold from the coin-producing cities of Dordrecht and Enkhuizen. Amsterdam was temporarily given the right to press coins, which it did in this former watch tower.
muntplein, tram 4, 9, 16, 24, 25 munt

(8) Photography fans will enjoy a visit to **FOAM**, Amsterdam's photography museum. Expect to see works by big names like Man Ray and Lee Miller, but also lesser known talents are also given the change to display their work. The museum displays historical and contemporary work.
keizersgracht 609, phone 020 551 65 00, www.foam.nl, open sat-wed 10.00-18.00, thu-fri 10.00-21.00, admission € 7, tram 16, 24, 25 keizersgracht

(9) **Museum van Loon** is located in a 1672 house on the canal. There's a collection of portraits as well as signed 18th century furniture, porcelain and silver. Behind the museum is a large garden in French style and an impressive coach house.
keizersgracht 672, phone 020 624 52 55, www.museumvanloon.nl, open daily (except tuesday) 11.00-17.00, admission € 6, tram 16, 24, 25 keizersgracht

(14) The **Magere Brug** (skinny bridge), a draw bridge, is one of the most beautiful bridges in Amsterdam and beautifully illuminated at night with hundreds of bulbs. The wealthy sisters Mager, who were both living on one side of the river Amstel, had the bridge built so that it was easier for them to visit each other.
amstel, between the keizersgracht and the prinsengracht (kerkstraat extension), tram 4 prinsengracht

(21) To be honest, Amsterdam legendary folksinger **Andre Hazes**, who died in 2004, deserves something better than the statue he's got, but anyway. Born in neighbouring Gerard Doustraat, Hazes shifted the epicentre of the Amsterdam folk song away from the Jordaan, where it used to be. Dedicated fans pay their respects and leave flowers at his statue.
albert cuypstraat, corner eerste sweelinckstraat, tram 4 stadhouderskade

Places to eat & drink

③ For many years **Van Dobben** has been the place for the most delicious sandwiches in Amsterdam, maybe even the whole country. Try the sandwich with croquet, the warm meat with peanut sauce, the roast beef or the meat sandwich. The friendly, witty service makes Van Dobben a fun experience that is typically Amsterdam.
korte reguliersdwarsstrat 5, phone 020 624 42 00, open mon-thu 09.30-01.00, fri-sat 09.30-02.00, sun 11.00-20.00, price € 4.50, tram 4, 9, 14 rembrandtplein

④ **Café Schiller** distinguishes itself from other bars on Rembrandtplein with its original art-deco interior and rather special atmosphere: Schiller has style and it's a good place for a drink before or after a visit to the Tuschinski cinema or De Kleine Komedie (Small Comedy) theatre. Both the snacks and meals in the restaurant are well above average.
rembrandtplein 26, phone 020 624 98 46, open sun-thu 16.00-01.00, fri-sat 16.00-03.00, price € 30, tram 4, 9, 14 rembrandtplein

⑤ A little piece of Paris in the heart of Amsterdam. At **Flo** you can get traditional steak tartare, delicious fruit de mer or a fragrant onion soup. Add to that the good wine menu and excellent service, and you're in 7th heaven.
amstelstraat 9, phone 020 890 47 57, open 12.00-15.00 and 17.30-23.00, during the weekend no lunch available, price € 35, tram 4, 9, 14 rembrandtplein

⑥ **Herrie** was top chef Herman den Blijker's first restaurant in the capital and was the setting for his television show, 'Herman seeks a chef'. Now the camera crew has disappeared, guests are coming back for the high quality dinner and cosy little bar.
utrechtsestraat 30a, phone 020 622 08 38, open mon-sat 18.00-22.00, price € 49, tram 4, 9, 14 rembrandtplein

⑯ **Amstelhaven** lies on a beautiful spot on the water. Ideal for lunch or a drink or evening 'borrel' snack. The crowd, most of them in their thirties, comes here after work. Later in the evening the music's turned up and the dancing starts.
mauritskade 1, phone 020 665 26 72, open sun-thu 11.00-01.00, fri-sat 11.00-03.00, price € 32, tram 7, 10 weesperpplein

22

5

(17) Don't expect culinary masterpieces at the **IJsbreker** (Ice Breaker), but this is still a great place for a drink. During the summer especially, you can sit on the lovely, large terrace and enjoy the beautiful view over the river Amstel.
weesperzijde 23, phone 020 468 18 08, open sun-thu 9.00-01.00, fri-sat 9.00-02.00, price € 18, tram 7, 10 weesperplein

(18) **Amor Amor** is all about the famous Spanish tapas, such as albondigas, chorizo and tortilla. But then better, cheaper and with a better atmosphere than other tapas bars. This isn't really the place to ask your partner to marry you, but it's certainly one to fall in love with them while getting outside the delicious food and wine. Amor, amor.
ceintuurbaan 223, phone 020 379 28 36, open 12.00-01.00, price € 20, tram 3 van woustraat & amsteldijk, tram 4, 25 ceintuurbaan

(19) A tiny French orientated place hidden in an obscure street in De Pijp, at **Klokspijs** you can eat a classy meal for a reasonable price. The famous Dutch restaurant critic Johannes van Dam gave the place a 10, since then the place has been packed. And they deserve it!
hemonystraat 38, phone 379 28 36, open 12.00-01.00, price € 20, tram 3 amsteldijk, tram 4, 25 ceintuurbaan

(22) Rotterdammers are already familiar with restaurant **Bazar** in their own city. And now this Arab-Turkish concept has hit the capital, too. This large 'Kasbah' offers fresh mint tea, Turkish beer and Arab grill platters. Plenty of food for very little money.
albert cuypstraat 182, phone 020 675 05 44, open 11.00-01.00, fri-sat 11.00-02.00, price € 18, tram 16, 24 albert cuypstraat

(23) At the **Chocolate Bar** it's all about seeing and being seen in this 60s/70s interior. Mingle with the beautiful crowd, order a cocktail or trendy snack like dim sum or typically Dutch Van Dobbe bitterballen (deep fried balls – they're better than they sound!). The bench outside is a favourite spot in summer.
eerste van der helstraat 62a, phone 020 675 76 72, open 12.00-22.30, fri-sat 12.00-02.00, price € 16, tram 16, 24 albert cuyp, tram 3 eerste van der helstraat

23

17

chocolate
23

16

㉕ CAFÉ KRULL

㉕ **Café Krull** has great sandwiches, a nice terrace, plenty of tap beer and a fine reading table. A peaceful oasis amongst the overabundance of trendy places in this neighbourhood, and therefore a favourite with many locals. *sarphatipark 2, phone 020 662 02 14, open 10.30-01.00, fri-sat 10.30-02.00, price € 12, tram 16, 24 albert cuypstraat, tram 3, 25 eerste van der helstraat*

(28) Ironically, there's a McDonalds just up the road from **Burgermeester** (a pun: 'meester' means 'master' and 'burgemeester' means 'mayor'), but taste-wise they're worlds apart. The standard burger is made from blond d'aquitaine beef, the lamb burger is made from lambs from the small Dutch island of Texel, and they also serve falafel burgers, Spanish burgers and goat's cheese burgers. Yummy!
albert cuypstraat 48 (a second establishment opens in the jordaan in the summer of 2008), phone 020 670 93 39, open daily 12.00-23.00, price € 10, tram 16, 24 albert cuypstraat

(29) Wood ovens are rare in this city, but that's how the best pizzas are prepared. **Da Portare Via** is a small pizza place where you order your pizza at the counter and take it home or eat it at one of the few tables outside. All ingredients are fresh.
frans halsstraat 63, no phone, open daily 17.00-22.00, price € 10 (only possible to pay in cash!), tram 16, 24 albert cuypstraat

(31) There are the most fantastic cakes to be found at **Taart van mijn Tante** (My Aunt's Cake), a lunchroom with an eye-catchingly cheerful interior. Mouth watering cakes! Always busy, always fun and famous from television.
ferdinand bolstraat 10, phone 020 776 46 00, open daily 10.00-18.00, price € 7, tram 16, 24 marie heinekenplein

(34) Wine bars are in right now in Amsterdam. **Boelen & Boelen** is one of the oldest and remains one of the best. Choose from a wide variety of wines, available by the glass or the bottle and to fit every budget. You can also have diner here or order snacks.
eerste van der helstraat 50, phone 020 671 22 42, open 18.00-22.00, price € 27, tram 16, 24 albert cuypstraat, tram 3 eerste van der helstraat

(35) No complicated creations involving macadamia nuts or caramel whirls. No, at **IJscuypje** you just choose between lemon, raspberry and pistachio ice cream.
eerste van der helstraat 27, phone 020 479 55 65, opening hours vary per season, price € 3, tram 16, 24 albert cuypstraat, tram 3 eerste van der helstraat

Shopping

(7) **Studio Bazar** sells everything you could need for the kitchen. From cutting boards to knife sets, from espresso machines to egg-timers. If you enjoy cooking, this is a place you shouldn't miss.
keizersgracht 709, phone 020 622 28 58, open mon 13.00-18.00, tue-wed & fri-sat 10.00-18.00, thu 10.00-21.00, tram 4, 9, 14 rembrandtplein

(10) **Concerto** is a CD shop with a huge and varied collection through which you can browse for hours. There's also a small second-hand department that will buy your old CD's. This is the place to find that rare CD you weren't able to download from the net.
utrechtsestraat 52-60, phone 020 623 52 28, open mon 13.00-18.00, tue-wed & fri-sat 10.00-18.00, thu 10.00-21.00, sun 13.00-17.00, tram 4 prinsengracht

(11) The window display of **Look Out** is one that attracts and passes unnoticed by few. They sell the ladies collection of, amongst others, Paul Smith, King Louie, Kookai and Bruuns Bazaar. Across the street you'll find the Look Out men's store. Both shops sell accessories such as belts, bags and jewellery.
utrechtsestraat 91-93, phone 020 625 50 32, open mon 12.00-18.00, tue-wed & fri 10.00-18.00, thu 10.00-21.00, sat 10.00-17.00, tram 4 prinsengracht

(12) **Jan** is one of those shops where you can buy almost anything. Books, interior accessories, bags from by young designers, belts, jewellery. The perfect place to find that perfect gift.
utrechtsestraat 74, phone 020 626 43 01, open mon 13.00-18.00, tue-sat 11.00-18.00, tram 4 prinsengracht

(13) Enter **A la Carte** and you have the world at your feet. This shop is packed with geographical maps and road maps, and travel guides for cyclists, trackers, climbers, divers and water sports enthusiasts, plus some beautiful travel and coffee table books.
utrechtsestraat 110-112, phone 020 625 06 79, open tue-fri 10.00-18.00, sat 10.00-17.00, thu 18.00-21.00 (only in july and august), tram 4 prinsengracht

STUDIO BAZAR
sinds 1967
7

CONCERTO
10

11

32

La Grenouille
12

DUIKELMAN
27

24

(24) **Tjins** is a world shop. Get delicious Surinamese sandwiches with pom, salted meat or cha siu, or buy a takeaway lunch box and enjoy your food in nearby Sarphati Park. As well as Oriental produce, there are products from around the world, from English mustard to American BBQ sauces to Mexican spices.
eerste van der helstraat 64, phone 020 671 77 08, open mon-sat 10.00-20-00, tram 16, 24 albert cuypstraat, tram 3, 25 eerste van der helstraat

(26) **Puyck Delicatessen** is about French sausages filled with Roquefort or lovely pungent cheeses that go perfectly with one of the self-imported wines. Just smell the olive oil. During the summer they also sell luxury picnic baskets for a romantic meal in Sarphati Park.
sarphatipark 34, phone 020 675 16 86, open thu-sat 12.00-19.00, tram 16, 24 albert cuypstraat, tram 3, 25 eerste van der helstraat

(27) Not just amateur culinary enthusiasts, but genuine professionals, too, know there's only one place to go to buy pots, pans, meat thermometers, steak knifes, lobster scissors, garlic presses and the like. The largest and best selection of kitchen tools is to be found at **Duikelmans**. The place, even if you're only a beginner in the kitchen...
ferdinand bolstraat 68-68a, phone 020 671 22 30, open tue-fri 09.30-18.00, sat 9.30-17.00, tram 16, 24 albert cuypstraat

(30) De Pijp could hardly fail to have a vintage clothing store, and indeed at **Mad Mix** you'll find original pieces, most of which have been used in movie and TV productions. There's also a small rack of new clothes.
frans halsstraat 35, phone 020 771 86 49, open wed-sat 13.00-18.00, tram 16, 24, 25 albert cuypstraat

(32) The **Kinderfeestwinkel** (The Kid's party shop) is without a doubt the most fun shop in the area. Loads of costumes, masks, reading books, picnic equipment, stuffed animals and other toys. A great source of inspiration for a children's party.
eerste van der helstraat 13-15, phone 020 672 22 15, open mon 13.00-18.00, tue-fri 10.00-18.00, sat 10.00-17.00, tram 16,24, 25 marie heinekenplein

(33) **Raak** sells interior accessories and other wanna-haves by quality brands. Check out the beautiful crockery, unusual bags and shoes, and beautiful photograph albums. There are even out-of-the-ordinary toothpastes and pedal bins. Everything is just that little bit different.
eerste van der helstraat 46, phone 020 670 42 06, open mon 12.00-18.00, tue-fri 10.00-18.00, sat 10.00-18.00, tram 16, 24, 25 marie heinekenplein

RAAK

Fun things to do

(2) The **Tuschinski Theatre** is a beautiful cinema in which to see a movie. Make reservations for a seat on one of the balconies in the main auditorium and before you watch the film, admire this unique art-deco masterpiece built in 1921. Tip: book a VIP- or love seat.
reguliersbreestraat 26-34, phone 0900 1435 (€ 0.34 pm), open daily from 12.30, admission € 10, tram 4,9,16,24,25 muntplein

(15) For a night out in **Theatre Carré** you need to make your reservations well in advance. This former circus, beautifully renovated in 2004, was originally owned by circus director, Oscar Carré, but since 1887 has become the country's most famous theatre. On its 100th anniversary it was granted the title 'Royal'. Check the website for programming, performance times and prices, or call for program details.
amstel 115-125, phone 0900 252 52 55 (open daily from 09.00-21.00, € 0.40 pm), www.theatercarre.nl, admission varies, tram 7, 10 weesperplein

(20) Stroll amongst the many stalls on **Albert Cuyp market**, listening to the bellowing stall owners as they tout their wares. Smell the fresh flowers, French fries, fresh caramel waffles, herring and spring rolls. This is also a good place to buy socks and other basic clothes. Don't forget to check behind the stands, where there are plenty of nice little shops and cafes.
albert cuypstraat (between ferdinand bolstraat and van woustraat), open mon-sat 09.00-18.00, tram 16, 24 albert cuypstraat

TUSCHINSKI THEATER 2

Rembrandtplein area, Utrechtsestraat & De Pijp

WALK 5

From Muntplein 1 walk towards the Reguliersbreestraat. Halfway down the street, you'll pass the Tuschinski Theatre 2. At the end of the street you arrive on Rembrandtplein where the world's best croquet roll is to be found at Van Dobben 3. At Café Schiller 4 you can enjoy a drink with the locals, a rarity on this square. Café Flo 5 is a little piece of France right here in Mokum (the old Jewish nickname for Amsterdam). Turn right into smart Utrechtsestraat and shop till you drop 7 10 11 12 13. Turn right into Keizersgracht for two interesting museums 8 9. Back on Utrechtsestraat you'll find a nice restaurant for the evening 6 before turning right into Utrechtsedwarsstraat and right again into Reguliersgracht. Between Prinsengracht and Kerkstraat is Amstelveld Square. Pass along the back of the church into Kerkstraat and then cross Utrechtsestraat. From here you have a beautiful view of the Magere brug 14. Cross the bridge, turn right along the River Amstel and admire Royal Theatre Carré 15. Cross Sarphatistraat and over the water via Professor Tulpplein for a quick drink 16. Here you'll pass the chic Amstel Hotel. Continue walking to Weesperzijde to discover a terrace 17. Cross the bridge to your right and you're in De Pijp. Walk along Ceintuurbaan passing a tapas restaurant 18 and turn right into Hemonystraat for yet another restaurant 19. Turn left into Hemonylaan. Ahead of you is Albert Cuyp market, where the songs of Amsterdam folk legend Andre Hazes are to be heard 20 21, and pass the Arab-Turkish food temple Bazar 22. Before reaching the end of the market, turn left into Eerste van der Helststraat to discover several bars and shops 23 24 25 26. At the end, turn right back onto Ceintuurbaan and then right again into Ferdinand Bolstraat for a cooking paradise 27. A bit further along you can reenter Albert Cuyp market, but you'll need to go in the opposite direction if it's the city's classiest hamburger that you're after 28. Turn right into the beautiful Frans Halsstraat for more great restaurants and shops 29 30. At Eerste Jacob van Campenstraat, turn right. Via Ferdinand Bolstraat walk, cake in hand 31, enter Marie Heinekenplein making for Gerard Douplein. Time for some more shopping on the way 32 33. Finally, on Gerard Douplein, stop off for a drink or even an ice-cream on one of the terraces 34 35.

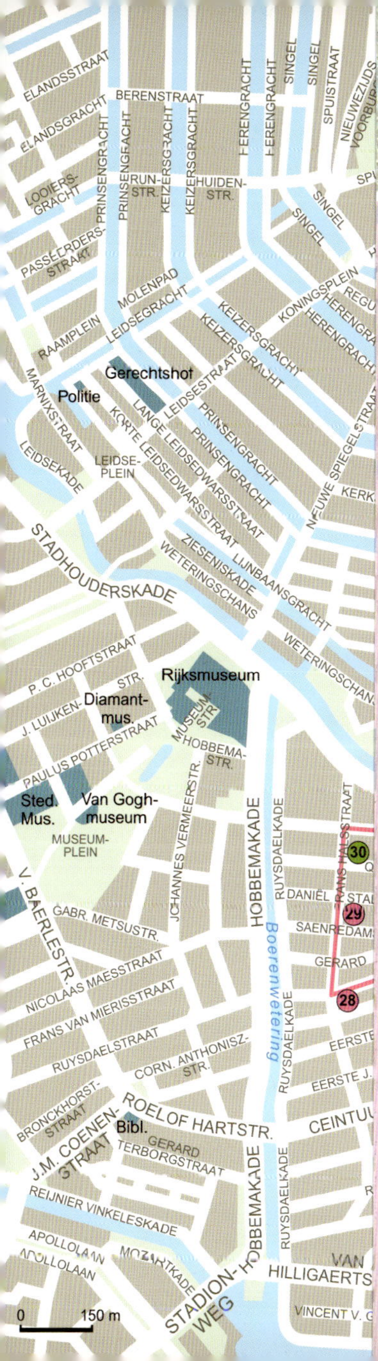

1. The Munt
2. Tuschinski Theater
3. Van Dobben
4. Café Schiller
5. Flo
6. Herrie
7. Studio Bazar
8. Foam
9. Museum Van Loon
10. Concerto
11. Look Out
12. Jan
13. A la Carte
14. Magere Brug
15. Carré
16. Amstelhaven
17. IJsbreker
18. Amor amor
19. Klokspijs
20. Albert Cuypmarkt
21. André Hazesbeeld
22. Bazar
23. Chocolate Bar
24. Tjins
25. Café Krull
26. Puyck Delicatessen
27. Duikelmans
28. Burgermeester
29. Da Portare Via
30. Mad Mix
31. Taart van m'n Tante
32. Kinderfeestwinkel
33. Raak
34. Boelen & Boelen
35. IJscuypje

The Islands

We all know the clichéd image of Amsterdam, as it's sold to mass tourists. The Amsterdam of the old canals, grand 17th century buildings, delicate brickwork, cosy bars and blunt, down-to earth humour of the locals. But a completely different Amsterdam can be found on the islands on the east of the city with their exotic names taken from old Dutch colonial days, like Java, Borneo and KNSM (Koninklijke Nederlandsche Stoomboot Maatschappij, or Royal Dutch Steamboat Company, which for many years was the main transporter of goods and emigrants to those colonies. Those glory days were long gone and the harbour of Amsterdam had moved when, in the 90s developers and the city began to transform the islands into what has become one of the hip, creative and increasingly liveable parts of Amsterdam. It is a place where architects have been given the rare opportunity to fulfil their creative vision.

6

It is a place where architects have been given the rare opportunity to fulfil their creative vision.

But there's more to be discovered round here than just the new islands. Another up-and-coming neighbourhood is the Czaar Peter area, where all sorts of interesting shops are also to be found. And a stroll along the Kalenderpanden is worth your while, if it's only for a free peak into Artis (Amsterdam's beautiful old Zoo) at the ibexes and zebras. You should also pay a visit to the Plantage area: an oasis of peace and arguably one of the most beautiful parts of the whole city.

6x what not to miss!

Centrale Bibliotheek

Centrale Bibliotheek (Central Library) to enjoy the view.

Muziekgebouw aan 't IJ

Muziekgebouw aan 't IJ to take in a performance.

KNSM-island

KNSM island for the interior design shopping.

Odessa

Odessa for a drink on the deck.

Brouwerij 't IJ

Brouwerij 't IJ for a 'Zatte' beer.

Artis

Artis a stroll round the zoo for the animals and the buildings.

- **Places of interest**
- **Shopping**
- **Food & drinks**
- **Fun things to do**

Places of interest

(2) The brand new **Centrale Bibliotheek** (Central Library) is Holland's largest and opened on 7th July 2007 (07-07-07). Visitors from outside Amsterdam won't want to join of course, but you should still pay a visit. The ultra-modern interior is beautiful and the layout state-of-the-art, but the real reason for coming here is the view from the restaurant on the seventh floor. A fantastic panoramic view over the old centre of Amsterdam.
oosterdokskade 143, phone 020 523 09 00, open daily 10.00-22.00, free, tram 1, 2, 4, 5, 9, 13, 16, 17, 24, 25, 26 centraal station

(3) The Stedelijk Museum (temporarily called **SMCS** - Stedelijk Museum Centraal Station) is located in this old post office building during refurbishment of the museum downtown. This is a strikingly appropriate location for the city's most significant contemporary art collection. The view from the top floor in Bar 11 is spectacular. The collection is scheduled to return to Museumplein by the end of 2009. (see museum website).
oosterdokskade 5, phone 020 573 29 11, open 10.00-18.00, www.smcs.nl, admission € 9, tram 1, 2, 4, 5, 9, 13, 16, 17, 24, 25, 26 centraal station

(4) **Nemo** is an interactive 'science centre' for all ages. Technology is playfully explained (lots of lovely knobs and levers!) to the (potential) reader of New Scientist or Scientific American. The roof offers a wonderful view and during the summer is transformed into a 'beach' on which you can enjoy a glass of rosé.
oosterdokskade 2, phone 020 531 32 33, open tue-sun 10.00 17.00, during holidays and in jun-aug also on mon, www.e-nemo.nl, admission € 11.50, tram 1, 2, 4, 5, 9, 13, 16, 17, 24, 25, 26 centraal station

(10) **Pakhuis de Zwijger** (Zwijger Warehouse) has over the years been used as a cold storage warehouse, a squat and a try-out stage for rock musicians (famous Dutch rocker Herman Brood used to practise here). One of the last warehouses left standing along this quay, it's now mainly used as a 'platform for cultural and media events'. There's also a nice café-restaurant.
piet heinkade 179, phone 020 788 44 33, open (restaurant) mon-fri 09.00-00.00, www.dezwijger.nl, admission free, tram 25, 26 muziekgebouw bimhuis

(18) It's worth a look inside the **Lloyd Hotel**, as this former prison provides one of Europe's more original places to spend a night. The lobby also has a café-restaurant which, like the hotel, offers something for everyone and every budget.
oostelijke handelskade 34, phone 020 561 36 36, open (restaurant) 07.00-01.00, www.lloydhotel.com, tram 10, 26 rietlandpark

(23) Windmills are not something one immediately associates with Amsterdam, but there are a few to be found in the city. The **De Gooyer** windmill, built in 1725, is one. Though unfortunately visitors can't go inside, it's still a wonderful sight in the city centre.
funenkade 5, tram 10 hoogte kadijk

(25) 'For now **Energetica** will remain located on the Hoogte Kadijk in Amsterdam's first power station. The future of this power station, which is a listed building, remains uncertain.' So says the website. Due to a lack of public interest and governmental financial support, the Energetica museum was closed in 2007… But we mention it anyway as it's such a wonderful example of industrial architecture dating from 1903. What a shame.
hoogte kadijk 400, tram 10 hoogte kadijk

(26) Each of the twelve **Kalenderpanden** buildings carries the name of a different month. They were built in 1840 as part of the Entrepotdok (Bonded Dock), where imported goods not destined for Amsterdam were temporarily housed. The buildings, squatted for a while, today provide 44 smart and spacious houses. The neo-classical gate, built in 1830, is also part of Entrepotdok.
entrepotdok 87-98, tram 9, 14 plantage kerklaan

(29) Espionage, helping people hide from deportation to the concentration camps, underground anti-Nazi newspapers: resistance in its various guises is the subject of the **Verzetsmuseum** (Occupation Museum). There's also a changing exhibition space focusing on modern ways of resistance against intolerance and suppression.
plantage kerklaan 61, phone 020 620 25 35, www.verzetsmuseum.org, open tue-fri 10.00-17.00, sat-mon & holidays 12.00-17.00, admission adults € 5, children 7-15 jr € 2.75, tram 9, 14 plantage kerklaan

CENTRALE BIBLIOTHEEK

23

NEMO
4

32

NOOIT MEER
AUSCHWITZ
34

(32) The **Hollandsche Schouwburg** (theatre) was built in 1892 as the fourth theatre in Amsterdam. During the Second World War the Nazis used it as a base from which to deport Jews and it's nowadays a monument to the memory of all the Dutch Jews murdered during the Second World War.
plantage middenlaan 24, phone 020 626 99 45, www.hollandscheschouwburg.nl, open daily 11.00-16.00, free, tram 9, 14 plantage kerklaan

(34) During the day, the small and intimate **Wertheimpark** is a delightful oasis in the city. Opened in 1812 as a present from Napoleon, it was one of the first public parks in Amsterdam where people could go for a walk. Nowadays it is perhaps most famous for the Auschwitz monument by Dutch novelist and sculptor Jan Wolkers.
plantage middenlaan, free, tram 9, 14 plantage kerklaan

(35) **Hortus Botanicus** is one of those amazing discoveries you can make in Amsterdam. This botanical garden dates back to 1838, making it one of the oldest in the world, and has an exotic mix of six thousand plants and over four thousand species.
plantage middenlaan 2a, phone 020 625 90 21, open mon-fri 09.00-17.00, sat-sun & holidays 10.00-17.00, admission € 6, tram 9, 14 plantage parklaan

Places to eat & drink

(1) You'll not find many locals at **Sea Palace**, a seven hundred seat restaurant heavily focused on tourist trade. But not so fast: with its wide selection of dishes from Canton, Szechuan, dim sum and many other Chinese cuisines, actually this 'palace' with its beautiful view is worth a visit.
oosterdokskade 8, phone 626 47 77, open daily 12.00-23.00, price € 24, tram 1, 2, 4, 5, 9, 13, 16, 17, 24, 25, 26 centraal station

(7) **Star Ferry** was named after the legendary ferry in Hong Kong. You'll not only find theatre and music lovers in this beautiful bar-restaurant, but anyone who likes a view while enjoying fusion food.
piet heinkade 1, phone 020 788 20 90, open 10.00-01.00, fri-sat 10.00-02.00, price € 30, www.starferry.nl, tram 25, 26 muziekgebouw bimhuis

(9) Hear the name **Fifteen** and many will naturally immediately think of the famous British TV chef, Jamie Oliver. But you won't find Oliver at work in the kitchen, but one of the chefs from a disadvantaged background that his restaurant trains. Large, out-of-the-ordinary, culinary, expensive, it may be; but it's worth a visit, at least for a drink. Jamie is OK!
in pakhuis amsterdam, jollemanhof 9, phone 0900 34 38 336, open 18.00-23.00, price € 46, www.fifteen.nl, tram 26 kattenburgerstraat

(14) Welcome to the old KNSM (Koninklijke Nederlandsche Stoomboot Maatschappij, or Royal Dutch Steamboat Company) departure hall. The **Kompaszaal** (Compass Room) on the first floor is a real unexpected treat. You can enjoy a drink here and, every third Sunday of the month, even dance the tango. And then there's the great terrace overlooking the water.
knsm-laan 311, phone 020 419 95 96, open wed-sun 11.00-01.00, www.kompaszaal.nl, free, tram 10 azartplein

(15) **Kanis en Meiland** can fairly be described as the favourite hangout of the islands' residents. But everybody's welcome here to play a board game or billiards, or just relax on the terrace with a beer.
levantkade 127, phone 020 418 24 39, open sun-thu 10.00-01.00, fri-sat 10.00-03.00, price € 15, tram 10 azartplein

KANIS EN MEILAND 15

⑨ FIFTEEN

(16) The **Odessa**, named after the Ukrainian city where this ship was built, is one of the islands' main attractions. On deck you can enjoy dishes from around the world, while admiring the phenomenal view. Downstairs it's more fancy and during the weekend some really great parties are often held here.
veemkade 259, phone 020 419 30 10, open sun-thu 16.00-01.00, fri-sat 16.00-03.00, price € 30, www.de-odessa.nl, tram 10, 26 rietlandpark

(17) **Lizboa**, anchored next to the trendy Odessa, is convenient - pay, grab a plate and serve yourself – and the Iberian-influenced dishes are amazing. There's also live music, so you can eat and dance to your heart's content...
veemkade 251, phone 020 419 3010, open fri 16.00-22.00, sun 11.00-22.00, price € 20, www.lizboa.com, tram 10, 26 rietlandpark

(19) Long live **De Cantine**, a down-to-earth, no-nonsense bar (and there aren't so many of those nowadays), where you can also get a simple and cheap bite. At the weekend you can enjoy an all-nighter then on Sunday afternoon get over your hangover with the live music.
rietlandpark 372, phone 020 419 44 33, open sun-thu 10.00-01.00, fri-sat 10.00-03.00 price € 20, tram 10, 26 rietlandpark

(21) Traditional yet modern. At the tiny but very pleasant **Helena Primakoff** you can enjoy breakfast or lunch. Try a regular brown or white slice with one of the less obvious fillings, like mackerel with lemon mayonnaise or humus with sesame and cucumber. Afternoon teas are also good. Choose between chocolate fondue and French toast.
czaar peterstraat 135, phone 06 48 95 90 94, open mon- fri 08.30-16.30, sat 10.00-16.30, www.helenaprimakoff.nl, price € 9, tram 10 eerste leeghwaterstraat

(24) **Brewery 't IJ** (the name of the water on which Amsterdam lies) is located next to the De Gooyer windmill and brews the best beer in Amsterdam (sorry, Heineken). Beer fans come here for a `natte´ (wet), 'zatte' (drunk) or one of the seasonal beers with names like 'paasIJ' (pun on easter egg) or 'IJndejaarsbier' (pun on New Year). A very friendly place with, every Friday at 4pm, a free tour!
funenkade 7, phone 020 622 83 25, open 15.00-20.00, www.brouwerijhetij.nl, tram 10 hoogte kadijk

(27) **Paerz** is a very welcome newcomer. The menu, above your standard pub food fare, changes every two weeks. There's always an exhibition from an artist and there are monthly surprise performances and so called jenever (Dutch gin) concerts. And all of this with a view over Artis...
entrepotdok 64, phone 020 623 22 06, open 11.00-01.00, www.paerz.nl, price € 25, tram 9, 14 plantage kerklaan

(28) **Café-restaurant Bloem** is beautiful located and has a wonderful terrace. Indoors it's also very comfortable in this trendy (but not too trendy) place. Top salads and great beef with port sauce.
entrepotdok 35, phone 020 330 09 29, open 12.00-16.00 & 18.00-22.00, price € 25, tram 9, 14 plantage kerklaan

(31) **Meneer Nilsson** (Mr. Nilsson) is named after the monkey of Swedish children's book heroine, Pippi Longstocking. But you don't come here for Scandinavian cuisine, but for the great tapas and meals from Southern Europe. Relaxed, pleasant place close to Artis.
plantage kerklaan 41, phone 020 624 48 46, open 09.00-15.30 & 17.30-23.30, price € 25, tram 9, 14 plantage kerklaan

(33) Not touristy and not hip. Just **Eik en Linde**, a legendary old brown cafe (pub restaurant), from which the famous Dutch interviewer, Ischa Meijer, broadcast his celebrated radio shows. Nowadays you get an eclectic mix of media people and their famous guests from the near-by TV studios, research biologists from Artis and the locals.
plantage middenlaan 22, phone 020 622 57 16, open mon-thu 11.00-01.00, fri-sat 11.00-02.00, tram 9, 14 plantage kerklaan

31

7

PAERZ
Timboektoe
Het productschap Paerz
adviseert genieten zonder
verordeningen, richtlijnen
27

28

28

12

20

Shoppen

(11) **Sissy Boy Homeland** is the interior shop of this well-known Dutch fashion brand. Trendy, but not too much so; certainly not cheap, but solid quality. Comfortable sofas, stainless steel four poster beds, scented candles by Dyptique, traditional Chinese toys for the kids.
knsm-laan 19, phone 020 419 15 59, open mon-sat 08.00-19.00, sun 11.00-18.00, tram 10 azartplein

(12) Don't forget your credit card. **Pol's Potten** has been the most trendy interior design location for many years for new residents of the islands. Collections from all the top brands and designers, you can also just come here for inspiration… and then go to IKEA afterwards.
knsm-laan 39, phone 020 419 35 41, open tue-fri 10.00-18.00, sat 10.00-18.00, sun 11.00-18.00, tram 10 azartplein

(13) Skaters of islands unite! The latest Vans and Etnies shoes and other street wear are all here at **Arrival/Departure**. In this small but well-organized life-style store there's stuff not only for the skating fraternity but anyone drawn by a good mix of vintage, bohemian chic clothing and wanna-have gadgetry.
knsm-laan 301, phone 020 428 72 29, open wed-sat 11.00-18.00, sun 12.00-18.00, tram 10 azartplein

(20) Go in search of treasure at **De Schatten van Jan en Joop**, a delightful and original little gift shop. The exhibition room for children's art is also very nice and for adults there's glass workshops.
czaar peterstraat 143, phone 06 270 77 848, open tue-sat 10.00-17.30, tram 10 eerste leeghwaterstraat

(22) Got an Arabian theme party coming up? Thinking of doing a belly-dancing course? At the cosy **Jeanines Souk** you'll find everything you'll need to re-enact 1001 nights.
czaar peterstraat 107, phone 020 420 55 72, open fri 14.00-17.30, sat 12.00-17.30 or by appointment, www.buikdanswinkel.nl, tram 10 eerste leeghwaterstraat

Fun things to do

(5) Need a bit of practice before that assault on Mont Blanc? At **Klimmuur Amsterdam** (Climbing wall Amsterdam), you can hone your skills even during inclement weather. Whether you're a beginner or more experienced climber, the 21 meter wall always turns out to be just that little bit harder than it looks...
dijksgracht 2, phone 020 427 57 77, open 13.00-22.30, sat 10.00-22.30, www.deklimmuur.nl, price € 10, tram 1, 2, 4, 5, 9, 13, 16, 17, 24, 25, 26 centraal station

(6) Luckily the **Muziekgebouw aan 't IJ** (Concert hall on the IJ) is more beautiful than namesake near Waterlooplein. Its Danish architects describe this middle-sized music venue on the water ('tIJ) as a glass business card. It's been the spiritual home of contemporary classical music in Amsterdam since 2005.
piet heinkade 1, phone 020 788 20 00, variable opening hours, variable price, www.muziekgebouw.nl, tram 25, 26 muziekgebouw bimhuis

(8) For many years the **Bimhuis** was in a modest venue in the city centre, but in 2005 the premier Amsterdam venue for jazz and improvised music upgraded to this wonderful location, which it shares with the Muziekgebouw and Star Ferry. There are over 250 jazz concerts per year.
piet heinkade 3, phone 020 788 21 88, variable opening hours, variable price, www.bimhuis.nl, tram 25, 26 muziekgebouw bimhuis

(30) It's worth paying a visit to **Artis** even if you've not got children to entertain. Aside from the animals, the zoo offers a delightful quiet spot in the heart of the city. Top attractions include the aquarium, the planetarium and the always up-for-it sea lions.
plantage kerklaan 38-40, phone 020 523 34 00, open during the summer daily 09.00-18.00 (and each saturday from june through august until sunset), during the winter until 17.00 admission € 17.70, tram 9, 14 plantage kerklaan

ARTIS 30

The Islands

WALK 6

Exit Central Station and walk past the bus stop into Oosterdokskade on your left. A bit further on you'll see a Chinese restaurant 1. Pass the library 2 and the museum 3. Turn left towards the water. For Nemo 4, you'll need to turn right and cross the bridge. Otherwise, you can already see the water and railway bridge. You can make a stop at the Klimmuur 5. Go through the tunnel and walk towards the IJ. Cross the bridge towards Piet HeinKade. Leaving Central Station behind, you pass the Muziekgebouw aan 't IJ 6 with café-restaurant Star Ferry 7 inside and, for jazz fans, the Bimhuis 8. Turn left towards the water at Vrieseveem. At the end of this street, turn right pass Fifteen 9. Turn left at the Jan Schaeferbrug bridge, with Pakhuis de Zwijger 10. Once you're on the bridge, you have a view that in many ways resembles Rotterdam. Take Javakade on your right and follow it until you reach Azartplein. You're now on Java island. Take a look to the left every now and then as you walk for views of the modern versions of the traditional Amsterdam canals. Time to go shopping: 11 12 13. If you need a break, try De Kompaszaal 14. Turn right towards Levantplein, then right again. After a drink on the terrace of Kanis en Meiland 15, cross the Verbindingsdam ('linking dam') on the left and turn right onto Veemkade where you'll find the boat restaurants Odessa 16 and Lizboa 17. The Lloyd Hotel 18 is a bit further up on your left, try Café De Cantine 19 next door. Walk through Rietland Park, passing the art installation, and on through the railway tunnel towards Czaar Peterstraat. Here you'll find a shop with children's artist's studio 20, a lunchroom 21 and the 'belly dancer's store' 22. At the end of the street, turn left towards the De Gooyer windmill 23, where the best beer is served 24. Turn back to walk through Sarphatistraat and Hoogte Kadijk past Energetica 25. Turn left into Entrepotdok for the Kalenderpanden buildings 26. Stop for a drink at Paerz 27 or Bloem 28. At Bloem, cross the Nijlpaardenbrug (Hippopotami bridge) on your left towards the Verzetsmuseum 29 and the main crowds on their way to Artis 30. Mister Nilsson 31 lies further down the road. Round the corner is a memorial to Amsterdam's history 32 and the bar Eik en Linde 33. Finish your walk at Wertheimpark 34 or Hortus Botanicus 35.

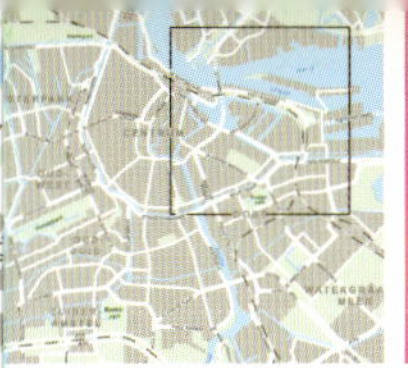

1. Sea Palace
2. Centrale Bibliotheek
3. SMCS
4. Nemo
5. Klimmuur Amsterdam
6. Muziekgebouw aan 't IJ
7. Star Ferry
8. Bimhuis
9. Fifteen
10. Pakuis de Zwijger
11. Sissy Boy Homoland
12. Pol's Potten
13. Arrival/Departure
14. Kompaszaal
15. Kanis en Meiland
16. Odessa
17. Lizboa
18. Lloyd Hotel
19. De Cantine
20. De Schatten van Jan en Joop
21. Helena Primakoff
22. Jeanines Souk
23. De Gooyer
24. Brouwerij 't IJ
25. Energetica
26. Kalenderpanden
27. Paerz
28. Bloem
29. Verzetsmuseum
30. Artis
31. Meneer Nilsson
32. Hollandsche Schouwburg
33. Eik en Linde
34. Wertheimpark
35. Hortus Botanicus

Places of interest outside the city centre

By following the walks in this guide you will come across a mass of interesting places. But there's more to see and do in Amsterdam than we can possibly describe here. To find out more, go to *www.amsterdam.nl* the official website of the City of Amsterdam or visit *www.holland.com/amsterdam/* the website of the Dutch Tourist Board. Some places of interest and areas not covered in the walks but worth a visit are briefly described below. You can find the letters given in front of the names on the city map on the first page of this guide.

(M) **Amsterdam Oost/Watergraafsmeer**, the official name of this district, is rather different. You won't find many stately buildings here and unfortunately there are some rather run-down areas, with buildings from the 70s and 80s that scarcely contribute to the cosy feeling to be found in other parts of the city. But Amsterdam Oost has more to offer than you might expect. It's just a question of seeking it out. The green heart of the area is the attractive Oosterpark, which is also the location for Amsterdam Roots, one of the best summer festivals of the year. The event is awash with the rhythms of world music and the aroma of Surinamese, Indonesian and other exotic cooking. Hotel Arena is located just round the corner: hotel, restaurant, club, bar and terrace this has for many years been a trendy oasis in this part of the city.

But above all, this part of Amsterdam is renowned for its multicultural atmosphere and it can hardly be a coincidence that the unrivalled Tropenmuseum (Tropics Museum) is located here. Javastraat is a classic example of multicultural Amsterdam. Here you'll find Turkish gift shops, sewing workshops, Halal butchers, Surinamese grocery shops and dotted amongst them here and there traditional Dutch high street favourites like Blokker and Zeeman. Then there's Dappermarkt, the cheapest market in Amsterdam. While in other parts of the city the house prices are soaring, here you can still find pleasant affordable housing. Which is why increasing numbers of double-income couples are gravitating to the east of the city. As a result, more and more tapas restaurants and other nice places are springing up everywhere, which in turn is a welcome for the local economy.

Particularly on the short east side of Oosterpark, you can find places serving really delicious food. In short, just the sort of neighbourhood you'll be reading about in lifestyle magazines in five to ten years' time.
tram 9 linnaeusstraat, tram 3, 7 muiderpoortstation

Ⓝ The **Amsterdam ArenA** stadium, home of AFC (Amsterdamsche Football Club) Ajax, is located a bit away from the city centre. Not that that matters to the true Ajax or other football fan. The guided tour 'World of Ajax' takes you along the pitch, the main grandstand and the press conference room. Those wanting more can visit the accompanying Ajax Museum, where more than one hundred years of club history is on display, including the first games from around 1900, the legendary European Cup matches, pictures, cups, trophies and personal items of Ajax legends.
arena boulevard 29 (Ajax stadium), phone 020 311 16 36, www.amsterdamarena.nl, check the website for variable opening hours and guided tours, admission € 9, age 5-8 € 8, metro 54 strandvliet arena or bijlmer

Ⓞ Anyone wanting to get away from the city's hustle and bustle can take a bike or bus to the **Amsterdamse Bos**, a nature and recreation park lying between Amsterdam and Amstelveen. On the border of the park are hockey and football fields and a major rowing club where races are regularly held on the competition course 'Bosbaan'. A cycle or walk through this park is quite delightful. Kids will love the goat farm and pancake house. The big pond is perfect for a canoe or pedalo ride and there are two children's swimming pools. The popular open-air theatre is a major and unique cultural event every summer during July and August. Attracting large crowds every evening, the atmosphere is highly sociable, with people often arriving long before the play starts and installing themselves on one of the benches with picnic baskets and bottles of wine. Arrive early and don't forget your corkscrew!
bosbaan 5, phone 020 545 61 00, www.amsterdamsebos.nl, free, the visitor centre is open between 12.00-17.00, bus 170, 172 bus stop van nijenrodeweg/amstelveenseweg (leaving from central station)

Going out

When it comes to going out, Amsterdam offers a world of possibilities. Film, theatre, music, dance or comedy: you can find it all. For an extensive overview check **PS**, the Saturday supplement in Amsterdam's newspaper **Het Parool**, or the free bi-weekly magazine **NL20**. The Amsterdam **Uitburo**, on the corner of Leidseplein and Marnixstraat, (open Mon-Wed & Fri-Sat 10.00-18.00, Thu 10.00-21.00) is also a handy starting point. Besides cultural information, you can also buy concert tickets here, sometimes even last minute ones at half-price. An overview of the main Amsterdam cultural festivals is given on **page 5 and 6**.

Listed below you'll find our selection of the many bars and clubs in Amsterdam. Each address is tagged with a letter corresponding to that letter on the general map at the front of the guide. To avoid disappointment, it's worth checking what's on that evening. Also keep an eye out for club flyers in record shops and other bars and shops.

(P) In its five years of existence, bar/club **Bitterzoet** (Bittersweet) has quickly built up a name as one of Amsterdam's leading clubs. Superb djs, a good vibe, an interesting ever-changing programme and just enough room for surprises make this not-so-big bar/club an ideal place for a great night of partying.
spuistraat 2, phone 020 521 30 01, www.bitterzoet.com, open sun-thu 20.00-03.00, fri-sat 20.00--04.00, tram 1, 2, 5, 13, 17 nieuwezijds kolk

(Q) Jazz café **Alto** is one of Amsterdam's best jazz cafés. Every Wednesday night the famous Dutch saxophonist Hans Dulfer hits the stage of this intimate and friendly bar. On other nights you can enjoy other famous and less famous performers doing their thing.
korte leidsedwarsstraat 115, phone 020 6263249, www.jazz-cafe-alto.nl, open sun-thu 21.00-03.00, fri-sat 21.00-04.00, free, tram 1, 2, 5, 7, 10 leidseplein

PARADISO (R)

(R) **Paradiso** is in a neo-Gothic church and offers something different every night of the week: jazz, fusion, latin, funk, garage, ska, deep soul... Very popular is the 'Classic Noodlanding' (Classic Emergency Landing) on Wednesday nights with live performances, cabaret and new disco. Every now and then, Paradiso also hosts big-name concerts. The Rolling Stones, David Bowie, Prince and Lenny Kravitz are just some of the artists who've performed here.

weteringschans 6-8, phone 020 626 45 21, www.paradiso.nl, open wed-thu 23.00-03.00, fri-sat 00.00-04.00, tram 1, 2, 5, 7, 10 leidseplein

ⓢ For less mainstream performances try the **Melkweg**. Every weekend the two main halls (The Max and Oude Zaal) are absolutely heaving. There are often special events like the Jazz & Fusion concert, SupaSonic Festival and Amsterdam Dance Event. The Melkweg also has a bar, gallery, small cinema and video corner.

lijnbaansgracht 234a, phone 020 531 81 81, www.melkweg.nl, variable opening hours (bar open daily from 10.00, halls usually open from 21.00), tram 1, 2, 5, 7, 10 leidseplein

(T) In a former church close to Oosterpark you'll find **Arena Tonight**. The music in this coolly decorated dance temple ranges from house, club and R&B to Top 40 hits. If you want to stay the near the club, you can book a room in the neighbouring Hotel Arena.
's gravesandestraat 51, phone 020 850 24 20, www.hotelarena.nl, open fri-sat 23.00-04.00, tram 10 korte 's gravesandestraat

(U) Want to be seen in the hippest club in Amsterdam? Then **Jimmy Woo**, with its long queues outside the door, is still the place to be. Once inside, you're immediately hit by the club's decor. The walls are papered with gold foil, there's an amazing amount of Chinese antiques about the place and the ceiling panel has some twelf thousand tiny light bulbs. With top national and international djs, a great dance floor and a cocktail bar, at Jimmy Woo an amazing night is guaranteed.
korte leidsedwarsstraat 18, phone 020 626 31 50, www.jimmywoo.com, open wed-thu & sun 22.00-03.00, fri-sat 22.00-04.00, tram 1, 2, 5, 6, 7, 10 leidseplein

(V) In the chic **Zebra Lounge**, with its red couches and enormous chandelier hanging in the centre of the club, the various djs ensure there's always a relaxed mood. Two floors of latin, urban, house, disco and more eclectic music offer plenty of choice in this sexy environment.
korte leidsedwarstraat 14, phone 020 61 26 153, www.the-zebra.nl, open daily 22.00-04.00, tram 1, 2, 5, 7, 10 leidseplein

(W) **Panama** is a former factory building on the Oostelijke Handelskade. Your night can start earlier here with dinner in the club's restaurant before dancing deep into the night. The djs are good and occasionally there's live music.
oostelijke handelskade 4, phone 020 311 86 86, www.panama.nl, open thu 23.00-03.00, fri, sat 23.00-04.00, sun 23.00-01.00, tram 10 rietlandpark

Alfabetical index

index by theme

hotels

fun things to do

Dutch collection 100% guides

ENGLISH EDITION AVAILABLE

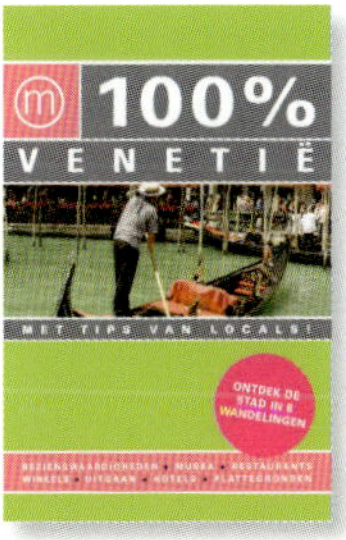

This guide has been compiled with the utmost attention to detail. mo'media does not accept responsibility for any inaccuracies. Should you have any comments, please post them on *www.100procentstedengidsen.nl* or send them to the address below.

mo'media, 100% amsterdam,
p.o. box 3936, 4800 dx, breda, e-mail info@momedia.nl
www.100procentamsterdam.nl

author revised edition	tijn kramer
author 1st edition	saskia van rijn
editor	marleen vos
translation	aryatti risamasu, gert verhagen, nynke westerdijk
editor translation	tom collingridge
photography	sven benjamins & marloes bosch
concept design	www.studio100procent.nl, naarden
design	jelle kos, zeal, zoetermeer
cartography	van oort redactie en kartografie, almere
lithography	mastercolors mediafactory, eindhoven
project manager	sacha kolk, mo'media
editor	wanda bakker, mo'media

100% amsterdam isbn 978-90-5767-325-2, nur 510, 511